"Readers will immediately recognize Kaytee['s] compassionate voice from social media, as she a[...] vors of childhood abuse and neglect. She balances clinical observations, research, and her own personal history to normalize and explain the invisible scars this type of childhood can inflict, and provides realistic strategies and practices to manage these types of traumas. Both lay-people and clinicians will find useful information in this book."

—**Robyn Koslowitz, PhD,** author of *Post-Traumatic Parenting,*
clinical director of The Center for Psychological Growth,
and host of the Post-Traumatic Parenting YouTube channel

"Kaytee Gillis uses her vast therapeutic experience and own personal journey to build a healing journey filled with compassion, practical tools, and hope. With insightful knowledge about how parental abandonment affects the self, relationships, and more—and powerful strategies to support healing in these areas—this is a must-read for individuals and clinicians alike."

—**Betsy Holmberg, PhD,** author of *Unkind Mind*

"Kaytlyn Gillis's book, *Healing from Parental Abandonment and Neglect,* is a revelation! She masterfully blends brilliant writing with research and her own challenges, creating an invaluable resource for healing. The transformative exercises—including coping with triggers, overcoming negative self-talk, and impactful guided imageries—empower readers to engage deeply with their healing process. This book deserves a place on every psychiatrist's and therapist's bookshelf, essential for anyone seeking personal growth or supporting others on their journey. A must-read for anyone ready to transform their past into a source of strength!"

—**Scott Shapiro, MD,** nationally recognized adult
attention-deficit/hyperactivity disorder (ADHD) psychiatrist,
and a renowned executive coach based in New York, NY

"*Healing from Parental Abandonment and Neglect* is a gift to survivors of this often-misunderstood form of trauma. Attuned to the survivor's experience by sharing her own, Kaytlyn Gillis guides readers on a journey to release self-blame, develop clarity and inner trust, and offers practical suggestions for responding to those who can't understand how a parent abandons their children. This compassionate book offers validation, supportive guidance, and a pathway to healing."

—**Diane Petrella, MSW,** psychotherapist, and author of
Healing Emotional Eating for Trauma Survivors

"Kaytlyn Gillis has filled a significant gap in self-help literature with her book, *Healing from Parental Abandonment and Neglect,* which focuses on meeting the needs of an often-overlooked group of trauma survivors. Her relatable and informative style, as well as practical strategies, offer an essential resource for survivors, their clinicians, and their families. I'll be recommending this book to my clients and colleagues."

—**Amanda Ann Gregory, LCPC,** trauma psychotherapist,
and author of *You Don't Have to Forgive*

"Gillis's writing is sensitive, nurturing, inspiring, and provides an easy-to-read guide to cultivating healing around developmental wounds. Inviting readers to consider how our families of origin can live on subconsciously in the present, Gillis brilliantly encourages the reader to psychologically liberate themselves from the familial shackles of one's past."

—**Mark Shelvock,** registered psychotherapist; certified
thanatologist; and adjunct professor in the grief education
program at OISE, University of Toronto

"Kaytlyn Gillis creates a transformative guide for defining and navigating the complexities of parental abandonment, showing that change and recovery are possible. Blending clinical wisdom with anecdotes and exercises, she empowers readers to heal their inner child and live more confidently as adults. Each chapter equips the reader with strategies to improve emotional well-being and find their authentic voice. I highly recommend this book to anyone wishing to heal."

—**Tara Overzat, PhD, LPC, NCC, ACS,** trauma therapist; *Psychology Today* contributor; and wellness advocate for resiliency, mental health, and climate change

"Finally! This is the book I wish I'd read when I was going through my own family trauma. Gillis has written what will surely be the go-to guide for making sense of a kind of pain that's not much discussed. Individuals and therapists should pay attention to Gillis's smart and warm insights. This book will absolutely change lives."

—**Jonathan Corcoran,** author of *No Son of Mine* and *The Rope Swing*

Healing from Parental Abandonment and Neglect

Move Beyond Insecure Attachment to Build Safety,
Connection, and Trust with Yourself and Others

KAYTLYN GILLIS, LCSW

New Harbinger Publications, Inc.

Publisher's Note

NEW HARBINGER PUBLICATIONS is a registered trademark of New Harbinger Publications, Inc.

New Harbinger Publications is an employee-owned company.

Copyright © 2025 by Kaytlyn Gillis
               New Harbinger Publications, Inc.
               5720 Shattuck Avenue
               Oakland, CA 94609
               www.newharbinger.com

Cover design by Amy Shoup

Acquired by Elizabeth Hollis Hansen

Edited by Kristi Hein

Library of Congress Cataloging-in-Publication Data

Printed in the United States of America

27   26   25

10 9 8 7 6 5 4 3 2 1   First Printing

This book is dedicated to all of you who have suffered the loss of a parent who neglected or abandoned you—my clients, my fellow survivors, and others. May you know that you are not alone, and that healing is possible. It was not your fault.

Contents

Foreword

Kaytee Gillis's new book, *Healing from Parental Abandonment and Neglect*, gently and compassionately leads survivors on a journey toward a more peaceful and healthy life. Gillis's book is one of the first to address this form of trauma and begin to provide knowledge for survivors so they can begin the healing process. Too often, the topic is not identified as a traumatic experience and an important clinical issue that may be the source of a person's suffering.

Gillis carefully weaves in her own humbling personal experiences to emphasize important elements of parental abandonment. Readers are given many opportunities to engage in evidence-based exercises designed to aid their journey as they revisit past painful experiences and their effects on their lives, ultimately aiming to rebuild a life where healing is not only possible but probable.

The book offers foundational support, such as creating a protector guide for venturing into troubling memories, and learning positive self-talk activities to change long-held negative and self-blaming thinking patterns. Gillis explains why survivors of parental abandonment often live with shame and self-blame, soothingly reminding them that being abandoned by a parental figure is never the survivor's fault, whether the abandonment occurred in childhood, adolescence, or adulthood. She emphasizes that caregivers are supposed to love and protect children unconditionally. As she states, "When you were abandoned, your caregiver broke the parental contract of unconditional love. You needed unconditional love, and its absence disrupted the developmental pathways in your brain."

Gillis delves into overcoming the shame that invariably arises from unresolved parental abandonment. An important aspect of her book is helping survivors understand that such abandonment can disrupt a child's brain development. Gaining this understanding fosters greater self-compassion and empathy. She emphasizes the cognitive dissonance that arises when the person who was supposed to protect you from harm becomes the source of trauma.

In detailing the consequences of parental abandonment, the book highlights how becoming aware of unhealthy patterns and actively working to change them can lead to a new self-view, allowing healing and healthier relationships to flourish. Whether the reader is a survivor or a psychotherapist working with clients who have experienced parental abandonment, this book is an essential resource. It can be used by survivors for self-help and by therapists as a therapeutic tool.

Healing from Parental Abandonment and Neglect not only provides trauma-informed insights but also focuses on building resilience. The book empowers survivors and gives them concrete strategies to replace unhealthy patterns with healthier ones, fostering a path to healing and growth. Ultimately, in a sensitive and trauma-informed way, Gillis supports those who have been abandoned by a parent by helping them recognize and develop an understanding of their history and work through feelings of shame and self-blame, and by giving evidence-based ideas to those at all stages of the healing process. This book is a much-needed contribution to the field of self-help and psychotherapy.

—Elaine Miller-Karas, LCSW

Introduction

Author's Note

The saying in mental health circles is that clinicians often base their specialty on their own trauma wounds: The therapist who specializes in disordered eating has struggled with it themself; those who specialize in anger management have personally experienced uncontrolled rage; and so on.

This is not always the case. I know therapists who have specialized in areas of mental health not because they related to them personally, but because they have developed a lot of experience and expertise.

I, however, am indeed one of the stereotypes. I specialize in family trauma because I lived it. I aim to help others heal from their wounds because I spent so much time and energy healing myself from mine.

This, dear reader, allows me to tell you with confidence that I know healing is possible because I have been through it. I have felt the pangs of despair, of longing for the parent who abandoned me to be there—holding out hope that he might show up for holidays, graduations, or other important celebrations—and I've felt the letdown and grief when I was let down again.

I am also here to tell you that healing is like riding a wave—it ebbs and flows. The waves may come at us like tsunamis at times, but eventually, they shorten and slow. The crest and fall may still be noticeable, maybe still catching you off guard, but no longer knocking you completely over.

It is possible to get to that stage in your healing, and you will get there. Support along the way will be essential, in all of the ways you need it. This book can be one of those supports.

How Can You Know If This Book Will Help You?

Perhaps the title of this book jumped out at you, so you picked it up. *Parental abandonment*, you thought to yourself. *Is that what it's called?* Maybe you opened it up with curiosity, wondering if you might have experienced abandonment or neglect, or *knowing* that you did and looking for further information about why it happened and how to heal. Maybe you believe an explanation of what happened could help heal the wounds you carry.

Surviving parental abandonment is a unique form of trauma in that it comes with a great deal of shame. This shame often keeps survivors from doing the work of healing. As a result, some may internalize their experiences, believing it was their fault and that they do not have the right to heal.

In my experience working with clients who have experienced parental abandonment, and from my own personal experience, I find that many adult survivors first start to confront their own history of abandonment when the effects of the trauma affect their current relationships. This can look like repeated failed relationships, difficulty with interpersonal relationships, or difficulties in parenting their own children that trigger insecurities and reveal hidden wounds.

This book is for anyone who has experienced abandonment or neglect from a parent or caregiver. Whether the person left physically or remained at home but checked out mentally, the fact remains that you were left to fend for yourself. This book is for all genders and all ages, but centers on adults and how the effects of abandonment often manifest in adult relationships and ways of coping.

How to Use This Book

This book is for anyone at any stage of their journey in healing from abandonment or neglect. If you are just starting to become aware of your abandonment, the denial slowly starting to lift, this book is for you. If you have been well aware of your history for years, maybe even aware of how it manifests in your adult experiences, this book is also for you. And for all of you in between, this book is for you too.

While it can be natural, and completely understandable, to want to devour this book in one sitting, I caution you to digest it slowly. The book is designed to give an overview of the road map for healing from parental abandonment and to help guide you along your path, but not to cure you completely in one reading. Healing never truly stops—this book can be a support throughout that journey.

In the early stages of healing, emotions and defense mechanisms are high, which can make it easy and common for any of us to forget what we have just read. As you read, you can bookmark, sticky note, or note in your journal the sections that stand out to you. Maybe you notice a familiar pang of loss or grief that arises at the start of a chapter topic. Note these sections to either return to and reread or save for later to digest at a time when you are more emotionally ready.

If you decide to flip to a chapter that calls out to you or to begin from somewhere other than the first chapter, this is fine. However, be sure to go back later and read the earlier chapters to ensure that you have a complete picture of the map of healing.

The activities and exercises in this book are meant to supplement your reading and provide additional support. Completing them is not mandatory, but I have heard from many patients and fellow survivors who feel their benefit when they follow the prompts to write out their thoughts and feelings. If you are one who finds support through writing, it may be useful to have a journal or notebook handy as you work through the chapters, although this too is not mandatory. It is also possible to use each exercise in a quiet moment of self-reflection. Pause, bookmark the page, and set a timer for a couple of minutes to reflect on the prompt or activity. However you get benefit and healing is the best for you—there are no specific requirements.

Because we are discussing sensitive topics, and traumas that likely occurred during your childhood or younger years, some of the sections in this book may bring up difficult feelings. This is normal. When reading feels too difficult, take time to reflect, journal, call a support person, and increase self-care. If you experience any negative symptoms that do not seem to improve, or if the negative feelings cause a decline in your ability to care for yourself, seek out a mental health professional.

The information contained in these pages, as well as the tips and exercises provided, are meant to support you in your healing, but should not replace actual mental health support should you feel you need it.

The case vignettes used in this book are all compilations of common experiences of abandonment shared by numerous survivors. All names and scenarios are made up based on this fact.

Part I

Understanding and
Acknowledging
Abandonment

CHAPTER 1

What Is Parental Abandonment and Neglect?

Neglect is as toxic as trauma.

—Bruce D. Perry, *What Happened to You?:*
Conversations on Trauma, Resilience, and
Healing

Maria was sixteen when her father moved out of the family home and went to live in an apartment across town. Maria was left with a mother who was depressed and slept most of the day, and two older sisters who stayed out all night partying to cope with the loss. The extended family, including her father, blamed Maria's behavior for her father's leaving, so Maria did, too.

"It makes sense," her sisters told her. "You two never really got along."

Everyone told Maria she was "old enough" to deal with her father's absence. She believed this at the time.

Without knowing why, she dealt with the resulting trauma by experimenting with drugs, engaging in sexual activities with whoever would give her attention, and eventually becoming pregnant at eighteen.

"Look what you did to yourself," her father said when he learned of her news. "You ruined your life."

His visits became fewer and farther between. Calls were never returned. Texts only occasionally. He refused to go to her high school *graduation, "embarrassed" to see her cross the stage with a pregnant belly.*

When she asked if he would be attending, he texted her: "You're an adult now. Go live your life." She never heard from him again.

Ten years later, she sat in my office. That baby that she'd carried across the stage in her belly was now the older sister of a four-year-old.

Maria wanted a better life for her children. She felt like it was finally time to process the abandonment she had experienced by her father's leaving. She did not want to pass that pain on to her daughters.

Understanding Parental Abandonment and Neglect

Few people in society would have blamed a two- or even three-year-old for their parent leaving them, but because Maria was sixteen, many felt she was old enough to bear at least some of the responsibility for his departure. When Maria's father blamed her behavior for his leaving, others reinforced this victim-blaming message and her already-developing self-blame and loathing. However, she and her father were not peers, but rather a parent and child with different roles and subject to different expectations of maturity and responsibility.

Children and teenagers are not mature enough to handle living on their own or bearing responsibility for their parents' actions. As an adult, Maria's father should not have blamed her for his leaving. But he did. This was what he felt he needed to do to justify his abandonment.

Most mature and psychologically healthy people would say Maria's father was wrong to blame and abandon her. We might also call his actions neglectful and abusive. His actions seem so unnatural that we might ask, "How can a parent turn off their love for their child?" The truth is, it's not natural. Maria's father was unable to provide natural love to his daughter because he was living out his own cycle of experiencing caregiver neglect and abuse, and this had a lasting impact on the young woman Maria would become.

When we discuss parental abandonment, we often imagine physical vulnerability—infants or babies in foster care come to mind. People commonly assume that young children are the only ones at risk of suffering the lasting impact of parental abandonment and neglect, but this is not true. Caregiver abandonment can be detrimental to a young person at any age. Teenagers need parental support just as much as young children do.

When that caregiver makes a conscious choice to remove themself from that child's life, by either physically leaving or checking out emotionally, this is called "intentional parental abandonment." Parental abandonment is different from other forms of maltreatment, such as emotional or physical abuse, but these other forms of dysfunction or abuse in the family are common precursors to abandonment.

Growing up without a caregiver is difficult, no matter the cause, but when parents like Maria's father purposefully abandon or neglect their child, this adds another traumatic burden for that child to bear. Maria experienced both neglect and abandonment: Her father physically left the home; her mother, on the other hand, neglected and abandoned her daughter as an effect of her depression, which kept her from being able to provide for Maria's needs. Maria was therefore prematurely thrust, unprepared and without a plan, into adulthood, where she was forced to fend for herself.

Most people consider mistreatment, abuse, and other behaviors or events that happened to individuals as contributing to their childhood trauma, but rarely do they consider what *didn't* happen. Parental abandonment is a caregiver's refusal to take responsibility and ownership of that role, to support their child's physical, emotional, and mental health. It can take the form of physically leaving or of physical or emotional neglect. In either case, the degree of neglect is traumatic and it can have long-term consequences.

The way we experience that trauma is not necessarily only about what happened, but also about how or what we internalized and learned as a result of those behaviors or events. Childhood trauma often comes as the result of a violation of trust and safety—feeling unsafe, as well as feeling unsupported and unprotected during these times of unsafeness. Children and young people with no other way to cope with trauma or make sense of it in an age-appropriate way often internalize it as self-blame.

Before our brain is fully developed, it is natural to internalize traumatic events as being our fault. This internalization then manifests as self-blame throughout our life. Even when survivors' behaviors and words convey the opposite—for example, a teenager may be incapable of self-reflection and believe they can never do anything wrong—they are actually internalizing that their experiences with their caregivers are their fault.

Add to this the pervasive victim-blaming messages from family, society, and other external voices telling us that survivors "must have done something to deserve it," and it's no surprise that observers find it hard to recognize parental abandonment. Because of that stigma, even survivors may take years to recognize the trauma of their own abandonment. But by noticing the patterns and behaviors in adulthood that are causing stress or other negative symptoms, we can become more aware of the effects of our parental abandonment trauma so we can learn to start dealing with them.

The Difference Between Parental Absence and Abandonment

"A friend in school often tried to empathize with me. 'I know what you mean,' she'd always say. 'I never knew my dad.'

"I smiled and nodded, even though I didn't think she knew what I meant. It was hard for me to keep friends, so I wanted to say the right thing.

" 'At least you got to know yours,' the friend would say, but I never knew how to respond. My friend might have grown up without ever knowing their dad, but how was knowing the guy for sixteen years before he left supposed to make me feel any better?"

When she described it, Maria would tell me how her experience always felt different, unlike what her peers had experienced. She could tell that her friend, who had never met her father, also had a genuine void within, but Maria's void was filled with self-blame, the good memories of her father, and the cognitive dissonance of feeling both.

How could the same person who taught her to hunt and fish just up and leave? With no other reasons but the ones she was hearing from those around her—that it must have been her fault that he left—she internalized this message.

Her fear of being abandoned again crippled her adult life. She stayed in toxic or even abusive relationships. Not until her second child was born did she realize she wanted to teach her kids differently from how her parents had taught her.

In our sessions, Maria worked on identifying all of the ways her abandonment manifested in her adult life: poor self-image, depression, binge eating, and an overwhelming inability to leave unhealthy or even unsafe relationships. For years, we worked together while she faced the pain that she had experienced through her abandonment as a teenager. Eventually, she started to feel the weight of some of the self-blame she carried decrease. Over time, she found she was worthy of love and deserved happiness.

Abandonment, like trauma, is never a competition of "who had it worse," but it is important to distinguish between absence and abandonment to fully comprehend the reality with which many survivors of parental abandonment have to cope. Parental absence is when someone grows up without the presence of one or more caregivers due to their absence. This can be the result of death, incarceration, or other involuntary causes, rather than the parent making a choice to not be there emotionally or physically. The absence of a parent alone is undoubtedly painful, with its own set of wounds and burdens to overcome. Much like survivors of parental abandonment and neglect, those who grow up with the absence of a parent often develop difficulties with emotional regulation and struggle with interpersonal relationships. However, this experience—one of growing up without a parent present for a reason that was not their choice—is different from parental abandonment. Abandonment and neglect, rather than being absent, is when the parent makes a choice to leave physically or refuses to do what they need to do to be there for you emotionally.

Abandonment *can* include physical absence, such as what Maria experienced, but you can also experience parental abandonment while your parent remains physically present. If you have been physically or emotionally neglected, you may feel the pain of parental abandonment because parenting is about so much more than just being around. In my clinical experience, I have seen an incarcerated parent put more effort into being there emotionally for a child than their spouse who is living in the same home, yet emotionally unavailable. This is not an ideal situation by any means—my point is that often the effort a parent puts into being emotionally present for a child matters more than their financial support or physical presence.

With abandonment, the effects are slightly but significantly different. Survivors trying to cope with intentional parental abandonment often develop severe attachment issues, such as an intense fear of abandonment and rejection and a wide range of emotional highs and lows, as well as profound struggles with their identity, self-compassion, and self-worth. Parental abandonment affects our whole being, our very sense of self, and can last long into adulthood, often leaving us with a pronounced sense of self-blame that manifests in everything from interpersonal relationships to daily social interactions.

This book is for all survivors of parental abandonment, no matter your parent's (or parents') reason for choosing not to parent you. If you had a parent abandon their responsibility to you—whether when you were a child, a teen, or a young adult—this book is for you. Most parents would describe their love for their children as unconditional and never-ending, but what happens when caregivers feel differently? Or perhaps they agree that parental love should be like that, but their own traumas and inner demons prevent them from being able to show it. To an adolescent or emerging adult who lacks the emotional and psychological tools to understand the reality of what is happening, the effects are still the same.

This lack of parental love can disrupt the formation of healthy developmental pathways. It can cause long-term damage to a child's self-esteem and affect their ability to form lasting relationships. For some, their trauma manifests years later—as a devastating breakup, emotional breakdown, or dangerous behaviors like substance abuse and risky activities that force them to confront the abandonment instead of pushing it aside, so they can get better.

A survivor's abandonment trauma can manifest in many different ways, but once they gain greater awareness of the possible effects abandonment can have on their life, they can take greater control over it. But before considering the events that led your parent or caregiver to abandon you, always remember: it was not your fault.

Common Reasons for Abandonment

This book is not going to provide an excuse for what happened to you, but rather an explanation, helping you to both understand what happened to you and, through awareness of its effects on you, develop tools to overcome it. The first step is understanding that each of our stories is unique. People can experience parental abandonment or neglect in their childhood, adolescence, teenage years, emerging adulthood, or even after they have left the family home, well into young adulthood, and they may still struggle with the aftermath and resulting trauma. They can experience parental abandonment by members of their biological family of origin, like a biological mother or father, or by parental roles filled in any other family of origin—whether being raised by their grandparents, two dads, or an aunt and uncle, or in a foster home or wherever they spend their developmental years.

The act of parental abandonment can also take many different forms. Some caregivers might pick up and leave their children; others might stay in the same household but stop engaging with their children altogether, shutting them out as a form of emotional and physical neglect. Abandonment can happen when the parent or caregiver leaves the house, never to return to the survivor's life, or when a caregiver kicks a young person out of their family home. It can also happen when a caregiver discovers the gender or sexuality of their LGBTQ+ child and emotionally turns away from them— existing in the same household but abandoning their child for being who they are.

Whatever reason your caregiver gave for their abandonment, again, it was not your fault. Even if they said you did something "wrong" at the time of the abandonment—such as getting caught skipping school or shoplifting, becoming pregnant, or any other adolescent transgression commonly used to assign blame—*it was not your fault*. While survivors might feel to blame for their caregiver's abandoning them, and a caregiver who leaves might even be reinforcing that message and blaming their children, the caregiver usually has other underlying reasons that drive them to the extreme of abandonment. Parenting can be hard, and undoubtedly it can bring out any individual's own trauma history. For their child, identifying the implied reason can help with understanding, But there is never an excuse for abandoning a child when things get hard.

Some who were abandoned never really got an answer as to why—it just happened. But if your caregiver blamed you for their leaving, you may have heard one of the following excuses, commonly cited by many of my clients (this is not an exhaustive list):

- Being punished for disclosing abuse or maltreatment inside the home

- Being left by the caregiver at an institution, group home, or somewhere else when caring for a disabled child became "too much" for them

- Being shunned and blamed by the family for coming forward about sexual abuse

- Being shunned for refusing to follow the family faith

- Being kicked out after getting arrested or dealing with legal issues

- "Coming home pregnant" and being kicked out for this

- Turning eighteen and getting kicked out because the family felt you were a financial burden and "it's time to take care of yourself"

- Coming out as LGBTQ+ and being kicked out for this

- Being kicked out of the home for engaging in a lifestyle caregivers did not agree with, such as dating someone of the same gender or different race or faith, having premarital sex, using substances, or any number of things that went against household rules or expectations, both implicit and explicit

- Being blamed for a family tragedy or crisis, such as the death of a young sibling or baby

- Being blamed for a parent's divorce

- Cutting contact with you because they "can't get along with you"

Similarly, you may have been abandoned after one of the following experiences:

- Staying with one parent after they divorced and never hearing from the other again

- Being forced to go out on your own after your parent moved, remarried, or invited someone else into the home and "no longer had enough space" for you

- Receiving a diagnosis of a physical or mental illness that was "too much" for your caregiver to handle

- Being forgotten about to the point where you had to raise yourself

- Being emotionally abandoned while still living with a caregiver who acted as though you did not exist

- Being left to fend for yourself while your parent left for another relationship, drugs, and so on

- Suffering abuse from which a parent refused to protect you, so you eventually ran away because the streets were easier than life at home

- Not being liked by a new stepparent after a parent remarried and chose their partner over you

- Leaving with no explanation

Childhood and adolescence are a time to make mistakes, even dangerous or silly ones, and actions taken during this time are no indication of who someone is or was as a person. This was a young person acting in a way that young people act. They were still developing, and if they made any mistakes along the way, whether legal or otherwise, they needed a parent to support and guide them through those mishaps or mistakes. Instead, their parents or caregivers turned their backs on them, reinforcing the message that they were to blame.

While some parents leave without assigning blame, often there is an underlying message, even if unspoken, that the child or young person was "too much" to handle or "too difficult" to parent or get along with, or caused some degree of stress for the parent who left. This self-blame can be one of the biggest obstacles to overcome in the journey of recovery from parental abandonment, but with greater awareness of how it manifests in survivors, we can begin to unlearn these behaviors.

Cognitive Dissonance: A Common Experience of Abandonment

Cognitive dissonance is the experience of having two or more conflicting beliefs at the same time. Enjoying a hamburger while believing that eating meat is wrong, spending money on an expensive pair of shoes while believing that you need to save more, and working at a job that pays well but challenges your values are some common examples of cognitive dissonance that many can relate to. It is when we have two conflicting feelings at the same time: We want the shoes and they make us feel happy, but we know we need to save. We know this company is not really ethical, but we also need to put food on the table for our family or children.

Cognitive dissonance is often experienced after abandonment when survivors have some positive experiences with or memories of the parent who left. Maybe your mother taught you to ride a bike or how to speak French, her native tongue; maybe she once treated your skinned knees after you fell. Yet maybe she also abandoned you when she discovered you were pregnant or had otherwise "shamed" the family.

I, too, have fond memories of my parent who abandoned me. We shared a love of classic rock and quiet evenings. We both struggle with small talk. I remember when he taught me how to write my name. When I grapple with his subsequent abandonment of me, in my college years, these earlier memories create cognitive dissonance, which can sometimes even feel like self-gaslighting. Thoughts like *Are you sure it was that bad? Maybe it really was my fault. What should I have done differently so he didn't leave?* are so common for survivors who grapple with cognitive dissonance. We know in our hearts that the abandonment we experienced was wrong, but we struggle to match the person who abandoned us with the person who was kind at times. How can it be the same person? It creates confusion, even reinforcing the feelings of self-blame for some survivors.

How can we have memories of someone who loved and cared for us at times, while acknowledging that they abandoned us during our time of need?

For those without any positive experiences of the one who abandoned you, I want to offer my sincere acknowledgment of your situation and validate your experience as well, which may or may not include cognitive dissonance. This lack of good memories does not mean that your experience of abandonment is any easier—or even that it is necessarily any more difficult. You may also grapple with cognitive dissonance that comes from other avenues. My clients who grew up in a culture or faith that promotes messages of honoring one's parents, no matter what, may grapple with cognitive dissonance because of a belief that they were wronged alongside a belief that they need to love and honor the parent anyway.

Still, there may be some of you who cannot relate to this experience, and that is totally okay. I do not believe that any story or experience is necessarily easier than others, only that they are different and each can provoke different results or experiences. Dealing with cognitive dissonance will be different for each survivor, but we should always validate it in all the unique ways it manifests.

Understanding the Cycle of Trauma and Abandonment

I want to give a little bit of background on some common reasons why parents abandon their children. This is not to excuse or provide any sort of empathy for them or their behavior, only to give some background for the cycle of trauma. Some survivors find that they do not want to know the reason, for they feel it does not matter. It's absolutely okay if you feel this way; I understand and support this position. As a survivor myself, I hold a similar position—that there is no excuse for what happened—but at the same time, I find it important to not continue the cycle of trauma within my family of origin and part of that involves learning a little bit about how the cycle manifests. No amount of explanation can excuse the neglect and abandonment, but gaining knowledge about this cycle is important for the purpose of breaking the cycle.

Often, parents who abandon their children are survivors of trauma and abuse themselves. Perhaps they dealt with their experiences by using substances, or they struggled with mental health symptoms of depression and anger. They may have grown up with their own internalized shame, which manifests in their parenting styles: Parents who experienced rejection as children may act in ways that are rejecting; parents who were shamed project that shame onto their children.

Parenting is an extremely difficult job and impossible to do perfectly. Such a stressful experience tests limits and brings inner wounds to the surface, including any shame or traumatic experiences from childhood.

Unhealed, parents use the victimized mentality from their own abandonment or rejection to justify abandoning or rejecting their child—they end a relationship or connection with their child because as a parent they feel victimized by something the child did. This is an example of an unhealed person who did not try to break the cycle—instead, they allowed it to continue. Moreover, a parent who struggles with substance use or mental illness but refuses to get treatment also repeats this cycle. Many of my clients tell me, "They choose drugs/alcohol over me," and I want to validate that experience. There are many ways a parent can choose abandonment over parenting, including substance use, mental illness, emotional abandonment due to being emotionally unavailable or disinterested, leaving voluntarily, moving away and cutting contact, and leaving physically to start a new life that did not involve you.

In a healthy parent-child relationship, parents have a significant amount of power and authority, and the child's position in that dynamic is otherwise powerless. This means the parent can never really be a victim of their child's actions within such a dynamic because the child can never really be at fault. Even a teenager cursing at their parents and acting disrespectfully is often a child acting out, albeit in an unloving and frustrating way, to verbalize their pain or discomfort within that relationship dynamic.

Of course, this does not give permission for a misbehaving child, at any age, to claim they are without any fault for their actions, nor should parents excuse or ignore them. In fact, parents should do just the opposite and address those actions, but remember that their child, at any age, is often the victim of an established dynamic and not likely to be responsible for it. In that dynamic, adults are largely the ones responsible for owning the impacts of their behavior.

However, an unhealed person, instead of taking responsibility for being the parent and adult, may project their unhealed wounds onto their child, blaming or justifying their abandonment. An immature or psychologically abusive parent, for example, would interpret misbehavior as their child's victimizing them. They may see the child's getting into trouble at school as evidence of the child's bad behavior, rather than a result of stress the child is experiencing due to family dysfunction. They then justify their rejecting the child as punishment or as self-protection against such "victimization." The parent who blames a teenager for acting out, who reports feeling victimized by their behavior, is likely to also consider themself victimized by a toddler who throws juice at them. These examples are children at different stages of development acting in age-appropriate ways to show their displeasure or discomfort. In dysfunctional family relationships, parents respond by projecting their own unhealed traumas, believing that they are being victimized by a child—the one who has limited power in the dynamic.

Again, parenting is undoubtedly difficult, but the child is *never* to blame for the stress and difficulties that the parent experiences while parenting. No amount of trauma or difficulty in one's background is an excuse for abandoning your own child. Parents are responsible for healing their own wounds so they don't harm their own children, yet the abandoning parent has refused to do this.

I wish to stress that when a parent abandons a child, this is not estrangement—it is abandonment. Estrangement happens when a child chooses to cut contact with a family member, usually a parent or caregiver, due to abuse or maltreatment. A parent cannot choose to be estranged from their child because the parent has entered into a commitment to care for their child. This power differential and the parent's greater responsibility mean that if a parent leaves or severs contact with their child—for coming out as gay, for example—they have chosen to abandon the child. This is not estrangement. Of course, there are some exceptions, but overall, the parent is not the victim of their child. So, if you have experienced a parent's abandonment of you, and this parent is then blaming you for the abandonment, please know this is not your fault. I offer tips and support for this scenario throughout this book, as it is all too common for too many of us.

I offer these basic whys and the hows behind abandonment as insight into how the patterns repeat so survivors can better understand some of the logic behind their experience. This is *not* to excuse the behavior or elicit any sense of guilt, rather to provide some degree of understanding. No one owes the person who abandoned them any remorse. That was their failure, not yours. And it is their fault, not yours.

As a survivor of abandonment, you were not protected by the one who was supposed to love and protect you. This was a failing on their part, and it is unfair that you were left with the burden of healing and overcoming. Part of this healing often requires us to do some reparenting of our inner child. This phrase, often used by mental health clinicians, refers to the act of supporting the wounded part of us in a healthy way. One way you can do this is through imagination and guided imagery.

In the guided imagery activity that follows, you will be prompted to think of your version of someone (or something) that offers you a sense of protection. This will help you begin the process of supporting, or reparenting, your wounded inner child who was abandoned.

Beginning Activity: Discovering Self-Protection

When we begin to learn about our history, it is normal to feel exposed, open, and vulnerable. It can sometimes feel like too much, especially if you have spent the past few years (or decades) thinking that you are not worthy of healing. As you move forward through healing, reinforcing the strengths you already have within you can feel empowering. These activities will help you realize and channel these strengths, giving you the support you need to move forward.

These two activities can help you create and reinforce self-protection. You can pick one or do them both. These activities are not mandatory, but know that they have created healing in many who choose to complete or self-reflect on them. Even if you decide not to complete them today, you can always complete them some other time. Moreover, simply spending some quiet moments in self-reflection about how you might complete them, such as considering what items you would use, can help give you strength and empowerment.

Choice 1

Draw or paint a shield of armor.

Items needed: A sheet of paper and paint or colored pencils, crayons, or markers

Time needed: From five minutes to as long as you need.

When you imagine a shield of armor, you might picture warriors in battle. Healing from trauma can often feel a lot like going to battle with the memories and resulting emotions. Just as a soldier or warrior uses their shield to protect themselves from danger, you will use the shield you create to help you overcome difficult emotions or experiences that may come up as you read this book.

To begin, outline a shield shape on your paper. Now think about whatever in your life you consider strengths—from personal attributes, like your love of art or writing, your use of humor, or your patience, to beings like a beloved pet, treasured objects, or any other support. Write or draw these things on your paper shield.

You can use these items on your shield while reading this book and any other time you need them. Call upon the items on this shield as you move through life. When you are dealing with stressful memories or difficult emotions, think about the items you chose and why, and how these items can help you cope emotionally. For example, if you drew a pencil because of your love of journaling, recall this strength as one of many examples of coping skills that can help you whenever you have a difficult time.

Some people choose to hang their shield up where they can see it every day—on the fridge or near their desk—as a reminder of their strengths and coping skills.

Choice 2

Draw or paint a box of protection.

Items needed: A spare, unused cardboard box or shoebox, old unused wrapping paper or newspaper, paint or colored pencils, crayons, or markers

Time needed: From ten minutes to as long as you need

We often use boxes to store items of value—memories, keepsakes, or other personal items. When boxes are stored in a closet or supply room, we may forget what is inside, open them to look, and feel flooded with the memories those items evoke. When healing from trauma, it is common to forget or "misplace" the knowledge of our many strengths, our memories, and the resulting emotions. Use this box creation to store your strengths and help you cope with the difficult emotions or experiences that come up as you read this book.

To begin, think about things that you consider to be your strengths that can help you cope. These can be anything—from the pleasure you take in gardening or hiking, to memories of a supportive grandparent or a beloved pet, to a trinket or souvenir that reminds you of your first solo road trip. Put these things into your protection box.

You can use the items in this box to draw on your strengths, both emotional and personal, when you need support while reading this book or at any other time. Call upon the items from this box as you move through life. When dealing with stressful memories or difficult emotions, think about the items you chose and why and how they can help you emotionally. For example, if you used a toy from a beloved pet or an award for a career accomplishment, these can help remind you of your support and strengths whenever you have a difficult time.

Some people choose to put their protection box out where they can see it every day, such as on or near their desk, as a reminder of their stored strengths and coping skills. For example, Maria could choose to use her box during moments when the negative feelings from her experience creep in. She could reach in and pull out a paintbrush, for example, to remind her of her skill and strength as an artist.

In this first chapter, we began part 1 of the book, starting the process of understanding and acknowledging abandonment. We went over what abandonment is and the difference between abandonment and absence of a parent—and how, while both can be traumatic, there are distinct differences between the experiences. We explored some of the common ways that abandonment happens, and, we stressed that it is never the survivor's fault for having been abandoned. We explored self-blame, as well as ways to recognize and unlearn it.

Next, we will go deeper into the pain of parental abandonment, as well as some of the common ways that survivors cope with their traumas. Many negative feelings will come up as a result of abandonment, and we will go over some of the common behaviors or personality traits that survivors may develop as they try to cope with their experience. You may recognize yourself in some of the following pages. This is okay; it means that you are on the right track—you picked up the right book! It can be difficult to read about some of the ways that you cope with your trauma; it can feel uncomfortable or even embarrassing. But it's essential to learn about yourself and your experiences—not to pathologize or shame you, but to boost your empowerment for self-healing. There will be moments of uncovering, but also moments of support and validation. All are essential to healing.

I am safe. What happened was not my fault.
I did not deserve to be abandoned.

CHAPTER 2

The Pain of Parental Abandonment

Can there ever be sufficient reason to abandon one's child?

—Abraham Verghese, *The Covenant of Water*

"He just moved away one day," Chelsea said quietly during one of our sessions. After getting arrested for public intoxication, she found herself sitting on my couch in court-mandated therapy as part of her substance abuse program. She was humiliated about her behavior and resulting arrest, but until this point in her progress, she had been quite guarded in therapy.

Like many parents who abandoned their children, Chelsea's father left when his daughter was still barely a teenager but old enough to have fond memories of him. She thought they had created a bond.

When he left, she internalized the anger she felt at his leaving; this led to self-blame and stunted emotional growth. Believing she had behaved badly as a child (for why else would he have left?), she began to see herself as undeserving of love or kindness. She abused her body with alcohol and other substances, not only to feel better in the moment but also because ultimately it made her feel worse—a punishment she felt she deserved.

When she finally opened up to me about another breakup with someone she had enjoyed getting to know, her anger, which she had carried like a protective shield, turned to sadness and flooded out of her.

With the wound reopened, she plunged back into a pool of self-blame: blaming herself for the relationship ending, for driving her partner away, and for anything else that came to mind. Her drinking increased and she struggled with interpersonal relationships.

In therapy, we again sought ways to work through this feeling of abandonment, spending more time working on her trauma history than on her alcoholism. As a relational trauma therapist, I knew she would be more likely to resolve the latter once she worked through the trauma that was causing her to self-soothe with substances in the first place.

Over time, Chelsea was able to develop better self-awareness of her situation. Through validation and acceptance, she learned to recognize the internalized feelings of anger, sadness, and fear of abandonment stemming from her childhood experience with parental abandonment and could identify when they were manifesting as emotional dysregulation and self-harming behaviors. She began to realize that, even if a partner did leave her, it did not mean that she was a bad person, and it did not mean she'd lost the only chance she would ever have to be loved. After spending so much time and energy finding ways to push it deep down inside, she realized she had never coped with her grief over her father's leaving. By finally letting herself feel the sadness of that abandonment, she could start to appropriately manage it.

Self-Blame: A Common Result of Abandonment

There is a wound that never heals in the heart of an abandoned child.

—Kate Morton, *The Clockmaker's Daughter*

The developing brain tends to internalize experiences, which is why children are naturally self-centered and relate everything back to themselves. This is normal development. When a developing brain experiences something traumatic, like parental abandonment, that young person is even more likely to internalize that experience, blame themself, and struggle with the resulting shame.

For survivors of parental abandonment, self-blame and shame often go hand in hand. You may have received the message that you're unlovable. If your caregiver blamed you for your behavior—getting into trouble, acting out, or engaging in any number of the activities that young people tend to try—your sense of self-blame might be even stronger. Even if you were not directly blamed, because you were a young person with a developing, internalizing brain, you might have received a message of blame, telling yourself *See, they left because of what I did. It's my fault. I am therefore unlovable, and people will always leave me.*

Survivors can carry this self-blame and inner shame into adulthood as deep feelings of defectiveness, damage, and self-criticism. It affects their ability to feel safe—in their life and environment, but also inside their own bodies. Deep inside, they feel unworthy of love. *Mom left because I was a bad child. Dad left because I am unlovable.* This may make them feel uncomfortable around healthy people or healthy relationships, believing *If this person knew the real me, they could never love me.* This internalized judgment and self-critical voice come from the deep-seated belief that they were abandoned because of *who they are.*

Parental abandonment can also manifest as fear of reexperiencing this abandonment in adulthood, making it common for survivors to worry that others will leave them—be they intimate partners, friends, or coworkers. This constant fear of being "found out" as unlovable and then abandoned can plague survivors during any interaction with others. After carrying this feeling for years, through many relationships and scenarios, it can be hard for survivors to unlearn. In fact, even just considering the prospect of living without this fear of abandonment might make them anxious. The fear can become almost like a protective shield that survivors mistake for self-awareness, thinking it will help them recognize and thus guard against the looming abandonment. Unfortunately, it does not work out this way.

This intense self-blame can drive many survivors of parental abandonment to develop insecure attachments, or patterns of relational bonds characterized by emotional and interpersonal struggles and difficulty forming and maintaining secure, trusting, and emotionally stable relationships. When you're convinced you are to blame, you may believe yourself to be irreparably flawed and unlovable. You might reenact the roles of your traumatic childhood or engage in other forms of self-sabotage in your relationships or work. You may notice that your history impacts your overall well-being: Some survivors note an effect on their mental health or daily mood, or even on their physical health and how they treat or view their body. Often, our behavior can unconsciously perpetuate any negative self-perceptions. For example, if we feel we are unworthy of love, this belief may show up in how we treat ourselves: what foods or substances we put into our body, or other ways that we may deprive our body of love and care. Many of my clients use substances, have unhealthy relationships with food or sex, and have other ways of perpetuating negative views of themselves.

By recognizing the connection between parental abandonment, insecure attachments, and acts of self-sabotage, survivors are better equipped to break free from such self-destructive behaviors and work toward building healthier relationships and a more positive sense of self.

Exercise: Recognizing and Unlearning Self-Blame

The first step to take in the processes of empowerment and healing from parental abandonment is raising our individual awareness about ourselves and the causes and effects of abandonment trauma—the more we know, the better our chances of healing.

It's not possible to categorize and list all of the ways that self-blame can manifest in adulthood, but I have created a list of questions to draw out some of the most common ones I have seen in my practice and personal experience. Read through the questions and note those to which you can relate. Keep an open mind, as some may be linked to your abandonment experience in ways that you had not previously considered:

- Do you often feel inferior, or "less than" others around you?

- Do you push other people away?

- Do you believe you are unlovable or "difficult" to love?

- Do you believe you were a bratty, poorly behaved, or difficult child and that is why your caregiver left?

- Do you believe your behavior and actions as a child made it difficult for your parents to love you?

- Are you a perfectionist or a workaholic?

- Does your inner voice become a powerful inner critic, finding fault with nearly everything you say or do?

- Do you struggle with poor relationships with alcohol, food, drugs, sex, gambling, or other addictions or risky activities?

- Do you hate your body, personality, or other things about yourself?

- Do you have a difficult time believing someone could really like you for who you are?

- Do you worry about getting close to others for fear that they will leave?

- Do you often worry others in your life will leave when they find out who you really are?

- Whenever something bad happens, do you automatically assume you are at fault for whatever went wrong?

- Do you often replay conversations or interactions in your head, worried that you said or did something wrong, or that others are mad at you?

- On the other hand, do you feel that you are never wrong, or do you struggle to admit when you have made even the smallest mistake?

- Do you often feel like you have to act a certain way to get others to like you?

- Do you consider yourself a people pleaser?

- Do you frequently compare your trauma to others', then feel guilty because so many have "had it worse"?

- Do you often find yourself in relationships where you are mistreated or even abused?

- Do you avoid relationships for fear of getting hurt?

You likely recognized some or many of the traits described in these questions as those you have developed as a result of your experience. You may have even related to traits you didn't know had any connection to your experience. Recognizing these traits is not about making you feel bad; it's about empowering yourself with knowing how your abandonment affected you as an adult so you can take appropriate action toward healing.

Next, read through the following scenario and imagine yourself in the same experience:

Think back to a time when you felt worried during a conflict with someone close to you. This could be someone you had just started dating or someone with whom you had been in a relationship for a while; a friend, or even a colleague with whom you enjoy a casual work friendship. It might have been a work meeting, a conflict with a peer, or a family holiday event—no need to remember the specifics or what was discussed, just the feeling of being stressed or concerned about the conflict.

Maybe, in hindsight, you recognize that you were afraid of abandonment. What in that scenario was happening that made you worry about the longevity of the relationship? Was there a conflict or another tension that you remember, such as an intense feeling of self-blame or worry? Take a couple of minutes to reflect on the feelings and sensations that come up for you in the process and/or write in your journal about what was happening and how you felt. It may help to use the following template as a guide as you write:

The first feeling or concern I remember was:

I worried that they would:

This situation made me feel that I:

Part of the healing journey involves recalling some of the difficult moments of the past to work on moving forward into a better future. After you reflect on this experience, it is important to remember you are safe now. In your journal or a notebook, write a few lines to remind yourself that, no matter what memories come up, you are safe and are worth this journey of healing. You might choose to write about your coping skills, all you have overcome, or your faith in yourself to overcome distressing moments. Write whatever reminds you of your safety and value.

Common Traits of Survivors

Faced with the option of feeling or not feeling the pain of a wound, most of us would want to skip over the pain. In the same way, survivors would naturally prefer to not feel the pain of their abandonment. This is completely normal.

But unlike someone experiencing the pain of a physical wound or a headache, for survivors, taking medicine will not remove the pain of parental abandonment. This pain will always be there, and survivors must engage in coping skills every day just to get by. Without a caregiver to model better behaviors, children often adopt unhealthy mechanisms to cope with their parental abandonment. For survivors who have yet to learn and develop healthy skills to cope with their feelings of emptiness and low self-worth, it is common to engage in substance use, binge eating, reckless sexual behavior, or other risky activities as distractions.

When young people are abandoned in adolescence or young adulthood, the place they believed was safe suddenly becomes unsafe. We are conditioned to fear strangers and "bad guys" from the outside—not people inside our homes, where we are supposed to feel secure and safe. Having a safe base we know we can return to is essential for our emotional and psychological development. When this cocoon of safety is ripped away from us, the trauma of abandonment can be everlasting. Everything we know—our sense of safety and security and our very sense of who we are—can be taken from us. No place can be considered safe if the one place we considered safe no longer is.

The survivor may then transfer that feeling to the outside world. Their developing brain learns that no one can be trusted and nowhere is safe. They don't yet know how to return to an emotional equilibrium, so they may remain in a heightened emotional state. Without support to help them return to their baseline, their nervous system develops under these conditions.

This is why you, as a survivor of neglect and abandonment, may commonly experience anxiety and hypervigilance, depression, and other mental health symptoms—some of the most common mental health results of abandonment. The extent to which these mental health symptoms will affect you may depend on your particular experiences of abandonment, as well as the amount of support (if any) you may have had in coping with these experiences as they happened to you. For example, someone who internalized their abandonment to a greater extent may have greater amounts of anxiety or depression than someone whose abandonment was noticed and recognized by another adult in the family who worked to get them help and support.

The U.S. Centers for Disease Control and Prevention (CDC) uses the term "adverse childhood experiences" (ACEs) to describe abuse, neglect, and other traumatic experiences that occur before age eighteen. ACEs are highly correlated with a number of mental health and physical health diagnoses, including several of the leading causes of death for adults (Felitti et al. 1998). The higher someone's ACEs score, the greater their risk for chronic illness and decreased life expectancy (Felitti et al. 1998).

For many of the patients who come through my office, their mental health diagnoses are a result of their ACEs. Many clinicians believe "child abuse and neglect is the single most preventable cause of mental illness, the single most common cause of drug and alcohol abuse, and a significant contributor to leading causes of death such as diabetes, heart disease, cancer, stroke, and suicide" (van der Kolk 2015). Childhood traumatic experiences shape our being and "the impact of major childhood adversities persists well into adulthood" (Schilling, Aseltine, and Gore 2007).

Trauma causes the brain to secrete stress hormones, which means survivors can spend years, or even decades, with their bodies functioning with elevated levels of these hormones, which can cause stress, anxiety, insulin resistance, and other medical concerns or diseases (van der Kolk 2015). With their bodies staying in a heightened state of stress, many survivors have a constant urge to self-medicate with food or drugs to ease the constant discomfort.

In addition, those who endure the specific emotional trauma of parental abandonment often develop similar personality characteristics. Understanding how parental abandonment shows up for you is important in order to begin understanding what areas of yourself need attention and focus during your healing process. As you read the following list, consider which characteristics resonate with you and take note of them in your journal. Remember, your ultimate goal is creating awareness to facilitate healing.

While not an exhaustive list, the following are some of the most common shared characteristics I have noticed in my practice and personal experience.

Fears of Being Abandoned by Others

This fear can be profound and pervasive, manifesting as desperation in relationships, such as being clingy or needy. Survivors with this fear might be acutely sensitive to potential rejection or abandonment, taking it very personally when friends have other interests, a crush doesn't return their affection, or they are not invited to a social gathering. As a result, survivors may have difficulties in forming and maintaining close relationships.

Fear of being abandoned might lead survivors to avoid being vulnerable with, trusting, or opening up emotionally to others. They might keep people at a distance, creating a self-protective barrier that inadvertently prevents the development of meaningful connections. Their fear of abandonment can drive them to go from relationship to relationship out of a fear of being alone, or to stay in unhealthy relationships past their expiration date because they feel difficulty leaving. They might also fear and avoid relationships altogether.

The heightened sensitivity to abandonment can also cause constant anxiety and an overwhelming fear of being unloved or unlovable. These negative self-beliefs can lead to self-sabotaging behaviors: unconsciously undermining their connections with others, pushing people away, or starting conflicts—all behaviors that discourage others from wanting to stick around.

Hypervigilance

Being abandoned by a primary caregiver during a person's developmental years destabilizes their fundamental sense of safety. In response to that profound trauma, survivors often exhibit signs of hypervigilance—an irrationally heightened state of alertness and sensitivity to potential threats or dangers. This can manifest as fear of people or places, or a constant nervousness or plaguing worry that keeps them feeling always on edge throughout their day.

This hypervigilance in relationships can manifest as a constant need to examine everything for signs of relational instability. They may overanalyze someone's words, actions, and even nonverbal cues for indications of an impending abandonment. Hypervigilance makes it harder for the survivor to trust others or believe in the stability of relationships, as they always anticipate that anyone close to them will eventually leave.

This deep-rooted need to anticipate and protect themselves from the emotional pain they experienced in the past can create a constant undercurrent of anxiety. A survivor's hypervigilance can make it challenging for them to relax and fully engage in relationships without the fear of impending rejection. They may emotionally distance themselves from others as a precautionary measure, believing that only detachment and isolation can mitigate the potential pain of future abandonment.

A survivor's hypervigilance might also affect their self-perception. They may become hyperaware of their own behaviors and overly self-critical. The perception that they caused their own abandonment colors every self-evaluation, contributing to feelings of inadequacy and a relentless pursuit of perfection in hopes of avoiding future rejection.

The body's constant heightened state of hypervigilance can also greatly affect a survivor's ability to sleep. Many of my clients report difficulty falling or staying asleep, often describing their body and mind as always being in a heightened state that makes it hard to relax and "shut off." Many survivors of abandonment struggle with sleep disorders.

Unhealthy Relationships with Sex or One's Sexuality

Often, after facing parental abandonment, a young person will become desperate for love and comfort from others but not know how to satisfy this need. When adolescents search for the emotional and physical connection they never received from their caregiver(s), they often turn to precocious sexual behavior (Ellis et al. 2020).

The abandonment experience during a child's formative years can prevent them from developing a healthy and secure sense of self, including their sexual identity. They may believe the only thing they have to offer is their sexuality, or they may not know how to give or receive love other than through sex. They may struggle with setting and maintaining boundaries in sexual relationships, out of fear of being abandoned again, and as a result, engage in sexual activities that betray their values or comfort levels.

To fill the unresolved emotional void from their abandonment experience, they may use sex to seek validation or love and enter into relationships only for validation, rather than to create a genuine connection. This may also lead them to struggle with intimacy and find it challenging to form deep emotional connections in intimate relationships. Fearing vulnerability and abandonment, they may avoid or sabotage intimate connections and emotional or physical closeness.

Decreased Self-Esteem or Sense of Self

Survivors of parental abandonment often struggle to develop their identity or to know who they are, be it as an individual or as a friend or partner. The absence of a primary caregiver during a young person's critical developmental stages can prevent their developing healthy self-esteem and a strong sense of self. They end up feeling a pervasive sense of inadequacy and unworthiness, as nothing tells a child they are unlovable more than a parent choosing not to parent them in the way that they need.

This diminished sense of self can manifest as a constant need for external validation. Survivors may seek affirmation from others to compensate for the lack of love and care from their caregivers, and the absence of such validation can deepen their feelings of self-doubt.

They may develop a distorted sense of self-blame, internalizing the belief that they were somehow responsible for their caregiver's departure and allowing that to define their value. Believing they deserve less than others, they may struggle to assert their needs, and they may tolerate mistreatment in relationships. They endure persistent feelings of guilt and shame for being the perceived cause of their abandonment, and their resulting self-destructive behavior feeds back into their perceptions of low self-worth.

Trouble Advocating for Themselves in a Healthy Way

Parental abandonment can profoundly impact a child's sense of worth and security and instill a deep-seated fear of rejection, making it challenging for them to assert their needs, preferences, and boundaries. After internalizing the message that they are not worthy of love and support, survivors can come across as people pleasers or even pushovers. They may struggle to express their needs and desires openly, fearing that it will lead to rejection or abandonment by others.

Survivors' fear that standing up for themselves might upset someone else can prevent them from being able to communicate assertively. To avoid potential conflict, rejection, or other negative consequences, they may suppress their own needs or opinions by engaging in a pattern of self-silencing. Believing that advocating for themselves could put their relationships at risk, they may avoid expressing dissenting opinions or confrontation altogether.

Conversely, some survivors overcompensate by being too aggressive. Their heightened sensitivity to perceived criticism or disapproval can make them defensive, overcompensating for negative feelings by being overly assertive. Their determination to prevent others from hurting them again can make them too aggressive, which prevents constructive conflict resolution.

Disordered or Addictive Behaviors

When parents or caregivers abandon their children while they are still developing, they often leave them without adequate support and ways to cope with their situation. Those children never learn healthy, appropriate self-soothing behaviors to deal with the negative and uncomfortable feelings that result. Without healthy coping skills, survivors may turn to anything that increases "good feelings"—like food, substances, sex, or gambling—to help decrease the negative feelings they have to manage.

Survivors of parental abandonment may engage in addictive behaviors such as compulsive overeating, excessive spending, or risky sexual behaviors, often as a form of escapism or just tuning out. In search of comfort, they may turn to food or other substances to help deal with their feelings of emptiness and low self-worth. Daughters of absent fathers are more likely to have disordered eating, be obese, or engage in addictive substances (Teachman 2004).

Like Chelsea, who learned to cope with grief over the loss of her father by self-medicating, most survivors only want the pain to go away. Drugs, alcohol, or other addictive behaviors can temporarily alleviate the emotional pain and provide a momentary escape from the overwhelming feelings of emptiness, anxiety, and unworthiness that may persist as a result of their abandonment trauma. However, these behaviors often send survivors into a cycle of shame and guilt that exacerbates their already fragile self-esteem.

Vague or Even Persistent Paranoia

People who were abandoned during the crucial developmental stages of adolescence or emerging adulthood often develop a sense of paranoia. To those who have never experienced abandonment, this feeling may seem bizarre and illogical, but it is common among those who were abandoned when they were young. They internalize this feeling of loss and project it throughout their life. When a child's safe base is rocked by parental abandonment, then nowhere will ever feel fully safe. When that safe base betrays them, how can they ever trust anything else in life?

Many survivors experience this feeling but often struggle to put it into words. It is a state beyond hypervigilance, a constant sense of being about to "lose everything." Survivors tell me they constantly fear losing their homes, possessions, families, or relationships, even with no logical reason to support the idea. But considering their trauma, this is normal.

In a child's developing years, the reciprocal and dynamic exchanges between them and their parents shape their developing brain. Unreliable or absent caregivers can disrupt those brain circuits, potentially resulting in cognitive delays, stunted physical growth, impaired executive function and self-regulation, and disrupted responses to stress. Severe parental neglect in the form of significant, ongoing absence of these interactions can lead to significant developmental impairments and threaten the child's health or survival (Harvard University Center on the Developing Child).

Abandonment greatly affects the developing brain, creating pathways and behavior patterns that stay with the abandoned child into adulthood. A survivor's brain learns to expect the unexpected to satisfy their need to always be prepared. However, rather than preparing them, it leaves them in a constant state of fear.

Fears of Having Children—or a Rush to Have Children

Childhood experiences like abandonment often influence our perceptions of parents and whether or not we even want to be one. Survivors of parental abandonment may report fears of having their own children. Many of my adult clients report wanting to avoid having children so as not to repeat the behaviors they experienced. Conversely, they may have children very early in an attempt to "prove" to themselves they are capable of love and of having a healthy, loving family. When I work with pregnant teenage clients, many report wanting to have the special relationship they missed out on with their own caregiver. All of these experiences can be a part of their ongoing attempts to solve or work through the trauma of abandonment.

Now that you have gone through the list, take a moment and rest. Think about the listed traits. Perhaps you recognized yourself in one or more of them. How does that feel, to see yourself described on the page in front of you? It may feel scary, or you may feel guilty. Ultimately, I hope that seeing the details helps to validate you—showing you that you are not alone and that these traits are common in survivors of abandonment. Learning about ourselves can feel uncomfortable sometimes, and this is okay. It also does not mean we have to try to change everything overnight—that's not practical or even possible! Rather, I want you to move forward slowly, with compassion and understanding. With this knowledge and understanding in mind, you can continue the process of learning and unpacking, which are essential elements of healing.

Parental abandonment is a unique form of trauma because the person(s) who was supposed to protect a child from harm and trauma ends up causing it instead. "Meaningful and connected relationships are a crucial aspect of development; without those relationships, children's development and well-being can be negatively impacted" (The Center - A Place of Hope). Those of us who have experienced abandonment often spend a lifetime trying to get a backlog of these essential needs met, often from relationships and those around us. This is not something we do purposefully; we may not even realize we are doing it.

Unfortunately, no relationship can take the place of the parent who left you; thus you may find that your relationships have fallen into the same pattern. Maybe they fail due to conflicts stemming from your abandonment wounds. Maybe you find that you date people who are wrong for you or even mistreat you, yet something keeps you gravitating to and staying in unhealthy relationships. This is a common cycle for survivors of parental abandonment.

Fortunately, acknowledging and addressing these patterns can offer survivors an opportunity for healing and healthier relationships. By exploring and reframing these fears, survivors can build resilience and a more secure sense of self.

Activity: Guided Imagery— Creating Your Perfect Protector

Take a moment for yourself. Close your eyes. Imagine your perfect protector, real or imaginary, who emulates all of the protective qualities you need. Who is this person or character? What powers or qualities do they possess that make you feel protected?

Some of you might already have a character in mind: a superhero or film or television character. It might be your higher power or someone who passed away and you believe now watches over you. Some of you might even imagine an extended family member—an aunt or grandfather, or someone in your chosen family. There is no right or wrong answer.

Think about this protector until you have a comfortable image or feeling in your mind when you recall them. Then picture them coming to you: enveloping you in a warm, supportive hug, telling you it will be all right; positioning themselves between you and whatever stressful situation you are undertaking; providing whatever you need to feel protected whenever you need it. No matter what, they always come to support you.

Allow yourself a few minutes to fabricate a scenario and fantasize in your mind about all the ways they will come to support you. Follow the short example provided—you can build on and change it as needed:

You just had a difficult argument with a partner or loved one and are feeling scared and alone. The negative thoughts and self-blame are spiraling: I'll never have a healthy relationship; I always get into these patterns; I can't get along with anyone; It's always my fault. These intrusive thoughts attempt to take over.

Then your perfect protector enters. They walk to you, place a firm hand on your shoulder, and pull you into a tight hug.

"It is not your fault," they say softly. "These things happen. All relationships have conflict, and it does not mean you are at fault. I know it feels like an argument is the end of the world, but you will be okay. You will get through this." They stay as long as you need, repeating a mantra—something like "You are safe, and it will be okay"— until you once again feel comfortable being alone.

The great thing about this guided imagery exercise is that you can use it any time, whenever you need it. Use it throughout this book, especially during chapters, sections, or content that provoke negative feelings, or at any difficult or stressful time in your life. Refer to them as your protector and draw them into your mind during times of emotional stress or worry. Imagine them protecting you in exactly the way that you need.

In this chapter, you explored some of the common personality traits found in the survivor community. Perhaps you recognize yourself in some of those traits. We also explored common ways that you, like many survivors, may have coped with your traumatic experience of abandonment, such as through food, substances, or sex. Hopefully, through this chapter, you learned that this is a normal part of the healing experience. I also hope that you learned how to show yourself compassion for these coping behaviors. As we go through the remaining chapters, I want you to practice holding that compassion for yourself, both as you learn more about yourself as a survivor and also as we unpack more of what the experience may have been like for you. Remember, your self-protection shield or box is there for you. Go easy, and take breaks as needed. You are doing great.

CHAPTER 3

Reducing Shame in Survivorhood

Shame is the lie someone told you about yourself.

—Anais Nin

Robert was sixteen when his father walked out of his life. Their last encounter was a screaming match in which his father called him a loser and declared that Robert would never amount to anything.

Years later, Robert began therapy after his boyfriend unexpectedly ended their relationship.

Robert sat on my couch, arms crossed in defiance. He remained silent after my last question, not unlike his response to many of my earlier questions.

When he first came to me, he said it was to work on himself. During his intake, he admitted, "I dunno, something just doesn't feel right. I'm angry all the time, but I don't know why." Since then, it had been hard to get him to open up.

"Well, let's start with what brought you here," I tried, giving him a lead-in.

"I'm just a bad person," he began. "I am always doing something wrong."

"What makes you think you did something wrong?" I asked, still leading, but tenderly.

"Because he just left! I thought the relationship was going well, but he just left. He said I have 'anger problems.'" Robert paused and shook

his head. "Obviously there must be something wrong with me because I can't even keep a boyfriend."

Finally, we were getting somewhere!

Those few words told me that Robert's inner shame was manifesting as a constant belief that he was at fault or there was something wrong with him, causing others to not want to be with him. It also gave me insight into how his trauma had manifested in mental health symptoms of anger, and quite possibly some depression and anxiety. Once I understood that, we could start to work on resolving those feelings.

When Robert was sixteen, his father walked out of his life for the last time. When Robert first told me the story, he said, "He was never truly present anyway, so I don't know if that matters." He had recently gotten caught with drugs on his school campus and was suspended. At his mom's insistence, his dad made a rare visit to their home. The meeting did not go as she had hoped; her visions of his dad talking sense into Robert quickly faded as the two got into a loud screaming match in the driveway, and then his dad stormed off. His last words to his son were to call him a loser and tell him he would never amount to anything.

What Is Shame, and Where Does It Come From?

Developing children and adolescents depend on their caregivers to validate and tend to their feelings and needs. When caregivers deny those feelings and needs or meet them with frustration, hostility, or criticism, the child internalizes that as themself being wrong or bad, and this generates shame.

Shame is an internal experience, though it often stems from external situations, like family-based traumas. The word "shame" might make us think of being ashamed—making a mistake, doing something wrong, a faux pas in public that left us feeling embarrassed. But unlike guilt, which comes from an identifiable source of "bad" behavior or "wrongdoing" on our part, shame is an overwhelming inner belief that we are fundamentally defective or deficient. The intense, inescapable feeling of being flawed, inadequate, unlovable, and unworthy makes us feel like we struggle for connection and never fully belong.

We can start feeling shame as early as infancy, when our caregivers fail to respond to our needs or expectations and a jolt of shame triggers distress. In a healthy home, that caregiver would realize and attempt to make up for their failure to respond, and although those brief shocks are painful, this communication exchange—the child expressing a need, the caregiver responding to the expressed need—both validates the child's needs and helps them learn about connection, bonding, empathy, and supportive relationships. When these exchanges and learning don't happen, a child can eventually feel shame about even *having* needs. With positive social support and validation, we can usually recover from those painful shame memories. When shame experiences are frequent and unresolved, however, we internalize that sense of being deficient (Bath 2019).

One of the surest ways for a caregiver to solidify their child's shame is through abandonment. Abandonment is a rupture in the parent-child relationship that goes unresolved, planting the seed for shame. This shame may well have become part of your identity and how you see yourself in the world around you. Your parents or caregivers were supposed to love and protect you against all else, to always be there for you. When they instead abandoned you, they sent a message: *Your needs and feelings are not valid. In fact, they are so invalid that I must stop being your caregiver, and leave.* Even though they did not say this message explicitly, this was the message your developing brain received.

To someone who does not understand abandonment, it might seem far-fetched that a caregiver's behavior could so severely impact their child, but early experiences of neglect, abuse, and abandonment result in shame at the core of who a person is. Howard Bath, consultant for child protection and youth justice services at Allambi Care (a human services provider in Australia), describes shame as "one of the more painful emotions because it arises when those most fundamental of human needs, the need to feel safe and the need to belong, remain unmet." Young brains interpret a lack of adequate parenting as evidence of their own low value and proof of their own defects. At this level, shame becomes "a painful, complex, and often destructive emotion that involves troubling feelings, a fragile sense of self-worth, and negative self-talk" (Bath 2019).

When your caregiver abandoned you, you likely internalized this message as *I was not loved for who I am. I must be flawed.* You may carry these messages with you, even in the back of your mind, not realizing at first that these negative internal messages arise from your core narrative of shame, connected to your abandonment. Even if you were abandoned as an older adolescent, college student, or young adult, this message is the same, no matter the age when it happens. The overwhelming shame we feel as a result of abandonment can shape our fundamental, unconditional assumptions about ourselves and our relationships.

Like many survivors of abandonment, Robert carried that shame throughout his life, believing he must be inherently flawed. He was abandoned by a father who was not capable of being a parent, who instead blamed Robert for his departure. Perhaps you can relate to Robert's experience of being abandoned by a parent who blamed you. I certainly can.

To avoid the negative feelings of the shame from your abandonment, you may adopt coping approaches, both adaptive and maladaptive. A 2019 review in the *Journal of Affective Disorders* found that toxic early childhood experiences (TECEs)—like physical or emotional abuse or neglect, originating from the nuclear family where the child's core emotional needs were unmet—typically contribute to the earliest and strongest maladaptive coping strategies. They also show measurable signs of increased risk of depression (Lim and Barlas 2019).

Robert believed his abandonment was his fault, and he often felt depressed and angry. His feelings were a normal result of what had happened to him.

The Ways Shame Manifests in Us

The maladaptive coping strategies that develop from the internalized messages of shame after abandonment can manifest in all the ways an adult survivor navigates their life—from relationships and friendships to otherwise harmless interactions with others. The shame messages can prompt challenging behaviors or constant feelings of anger, fear, hopelessness, and inadequacy. In Robert's case, as with many survivors, his shame created a defense mechanism of anger, both to release some of those inner feelings of shame and worthlessness and to push others away. This anger can manifest in many different ways in a survivor's life. They may react violently after getting cut off in traffic; conversations with car mechanics or delivery personnel may quickly turn ugly; or they may become known for being hot-tempered or irritable. Sometimes, in hindsight, we can see that our reaction was disproportionate to the offending event, but our actions at the time stemmed from our inner shame. Perhaps you can relate to the feeling of anger that came from being abandoned and not knowing what to do with it. Again, I know I can.

It's possible that you relate not to the feeling of anger toward others, but to the feeling of anger or pain you direct at yourself. Shame affects how we talk about and to ourselves, and how we treat ourselves. Perhaps you engage in derogatory self-talk or self-harm, or you withdraw completely, hiding from anyone who might compound your shame. Some survivors may attempt to override the pain of shame with substances or by doing excessive good and people-pleasing. Sometimes, we feel shame during moments of happiness and joy—when an inner voice creeps up to tell us to not be happy; that we don't deserve it. When we feel most in need of love or affection, having those human needs triggers that shaming inner voice. To avoid experiences that might bring up these vulnerabilities, many survivors avoid reaching out for the love and support they need. If you have a tendency to isolate or withdraw from people, this is likely why.

Here is a list of some of the common ways that shame can manifest in adult survivors of abandonment. Grab your journal, read through the list, and see if any of them sound familiar. As you read, jot down any thoughts in your journal to keep in mind as you move forward with the process of learning.

- **Perfectionism:** Survivors harboring shame from abandonment often believe themselves or their imperfections to be at fault, so they carry an overwhelming feeling that their work must be perfect or it will otherwise "prove" their shortcomings. You may relate to this if you've ever referred to yourself as a perfectionist. Maybe you've noticed that you procrastinate to avoid doing anything that might make you feel less than perfect. Some clients have told me if they cannot do it perfectly, they feel like a failure.

- **Constant worry about others:** In childhood, some survivors of abandonment had to worry about their caregivers' feelings. Maybe you had a parent who was inconsistent, appearing from time to time either emotionally or physically, only to withdraw again. As an adult, you may carry this same sense into other relationships, constantly worrying about what others think of you or how others feel. This feeling of needing to anticipate and manage how others think of us becomes almost like a necessity to ensure our safety.

- **Persistent negative self-talk:** When survivors of abandonment act in a way that feels imperfect or wrong—making a mistake at work, misspeaking during a presentation, or behaving inappropriately with friends or a partner—their constant feelings of shame, of being bad or wrong, can manifest as persistent negative self-talk to reinforce this feeling.

- **Depression, anger:** When an inner voice tells us we are bad or wrong, we either (1) internalize that message and believe it, leading to depression, or (2) develop a defense mechanism to "prove" these inner feelings wrong, leading to anger or aggression. Or we develop some sort of combination—for survivors like Robert, their inner shame can also drive them to vacillate between the two.

- **Struggling with self-esteem:** Abandonment gave you the message that you are not worthy of love and support. If left uncountered, this message becomes an internal refrain and may plague you into adulthood. As a result, many survivors will engage in a constant battle with their own poor self-esteem.

- **Disordered eating or substance misuse:** As John Bradshaw details in his book *Healing the Shame That Binds You*, compulsive and addictive behavior is closely tied to childhood trauma, particularly childhood abandonment. "We walk and talk like adults, but beneath the surface is a little child who feels empty and needy, a child whose needs are insatiable because he has a child's needs in an adult body. This insatiable child is the core of all compulsive/addictive behavior" (Bradshaw 2005).

I know this was a lot of information to take in at once. Maybe a lot of it made sense and gave you an "aha!" moment. Or maybe some of it seemed unfamiliar. If you can relate to any of these common struggles, know that you are behaving in a normal way due to what happened to you. But also know it is okay to have a different experience—all survivors will have different experiences, and no two will look exactly alike. Now we're going to learn some tools to stop this behavior and work through the shame.

Negative Messages from Extended Family and Society

Those abandoned by a parent are no strangers to shame and self-blame, nor to the negative messages from society or individuals that reflect these false beliefs. All of these negative messages we receive can impact our healing and compound the shame we feel. In fact, I find the negative, victim-blaming messages that many survivors hear from people on the outside can feel almost like another form of abandonment or trauma. In my experience working with survivors of family trauma, I rarely come across someone who's had the experience of being able to openly and honestly share their feelings with an adult in their family or even a safe adult outside the family. Perhaps having this experience would have helped decrease their trauma and the aftermath. I find this especially true for survivors of abandonment, who often find their experience excused, denied, or even flipped around to place the blame on them. I, too, experienced this. I remember extended family members reinforcing my father's abandonment of me by discussing how we "didn't get along." These words always hurt, because they reinforced the self-blame and shame I had carried with me for so long.

Unfortunately, society struggles with the concept of parental abandonment because it goes against what we tend to view as natural. This makes it much easier to blame the young child or even young adult when parents abandon them—a child acts out, and suddenly, society finds it justifiable that their parents "could no longer handle them anymore." A teenager comes out as LGBTQ+ and the parents cut ties because they claim that they "have the right to our beliefs." This focuses on the child's behavior as being flawed rather than on the adult caregiver's act of leaving. Perhaps this happened to you. If you were abandoned as an older adolescent or emerging adult, it's more likely this was your experience, although it can happen to anyone at any age.

Furthermore, society may have blamed you for the behaviors that you needed to adopt in order to survive the trauma of being abandoned. A teenager who is using substances or getting in trouble at school, for example, gets blamed for their behavior, often without a moment's thought given to what could have happened to lead to this. Perhaps this happened to you along your journey. Society, and maybe your external family or social circle, may have blamed you for doing what you needed to do to make it. Perhaps you are experiencing this now. If you are, I am sorry you are experiencing this form of victim-blaming. It is unfair to you.

When Survivors Are Blamed for Their Abandonment

Whether you are just beginning your healing journey or have been trying to heal for a while, you will undoubtedly be faced with many victim-blaming statements along the way. Some may come from extended family, who may not realize how their statements unintentionally reinforce the behavior of the parent who left. The uncle who urges you to "see it from their perspective," or a cousin who shouts, "But she's your mother!" may not realize the impact of their statement. Some statements may come from much closer: siblings or other family members may report feeling "in the middle," giving equal blame to the victim and the one who abandoned them.

Other statements may come from complete strangers, yet their words may impact you just as much. Insensitive comments online or from mutual friends can come across as blaming you for your abandonment. A social media post about "family is everything"; a colleague suggesting, "He's your father. Just give him a call"—all such remarks show an overall lack of understanding or compassion for the situation.

Of course, responding to others is only half the battle. The other half, as you may well know, is the experience within you—the shame, guilt, and self-doubt that compounds inside after hearing and responding; trying to make sense of how to explain your situation to others. The following is a list of common thoughts that may come up for you. Grab your journal, then read through and see if any of them sound familiar. Feel free to jot down any notes in your journal, or just keep them in mind as you move through the exercise. Then read the exercise that follows to begin learning how to respond to these negative messages from society.

Some common thoughts:

- *Maybe they're right. It seems so simple when they tell me to just call my parent. I should just get over it.*

- *When I tell the story, it makes me look bad. After all, my parents kicked me out after I got caught drunk driving. Maybe others will side with my parents if they know the truth.*

- *Why can't I just have a normal family?*

- *Should I just get over it? Everyone has family difficulties, right?*

- *Do I seem angry when I'm telling the story?*

- *They're probably judging me and thinking I'm messed up for having this history.*

- *In order to tell them, I have to reveal some personal family history. Am I betraying my family by doing this?*

Did any others come to mind? Add them in your journal.

No one knows how abandonment will impact them until they have been through it. That's why many of the victim-blaming comments will be from people who just do not understand. Their statements may sting, but I like to believe that *most* people are speaking from a well-meaning place and, perhaps, a lack of understanding. Of course, there will be some who fully side with or defend the one who abandoned you. These are typically people who have an interest in not seeing the person as having abandoned their child—for example, the parent who left gets a new spouse or has other children who may be engaged to do the dirty work of defending them. These, in my experience, are the most hurtful, and often the most difficult to respond to. However, it may be helpful to see them as having a vested interest in masking the trauma. Unfortunately, this means they have an interest in denying the truth.

In most cases, I recommend not engaging with people who refuse to validate your experience, who instead choose to deny your reality. However, there may be times when you are forced to engage with them, such as at extended-family gatherings like a wedding or funeral.

For these instances, advance preparation of some ways to respond to statements from others can help, at least to prevent some of the shame that comes from hearing them.

Exercise: Responding to Victim-Blaming Comments from Others

Read through this role-play scenario and imagine yourself in the same experience. Then follow some of the prompts for what to say when faced with victim-blaming comments from others.

You are inviting people to attend a highly anticipated celebration—a wedding, graduation, or other milestone event—and include people from work, friends, as well as some of your extended family. Since your parent who abandoned you is no longer in your life, they will not be there. You already know that other attendees will have questions about their absence—some well-meaning, others judgmental.

First, take a moment to reflect on this experience and how you feel about having a celebration where the parent who abandoned you is not there. You may feel sad or concerned, or perhaps you feel relieved. All of these are okay.

To continue, write down a couple of the feelings that come up for you in your journal or notebook. The key is to acknowledge and validate these feelings, as you deserve to have your feelings validated and supported.

The following are some common forms these questions or statements might take, followed by response choices. Read each question and try to match it with one of the responses that you would feel most comfortable giving. Write the responses in your notebook. For example, you may pair #1 with response choice E. It is okay to repeat some choices, or even to come up with your own.

1. Neighbor: "Why isn't your mother here? The mother of the groom plays a major role!"

2. Friend: "If your dad won't be here, who will walk you down the aisle?"

3. Friend: "That's so sad that your dad won't be here for this special day!"

4. Coworker: "You should just call them; they're your parent. They want to be here."

5. Friend: "I can't imagine celebrating such an occasion without my mother/father/parent there!"

6. Sister: "I feel like I have to choose between you and Mom if I come since she isn't invited."

7. Guest: "Shouldn't you have made up with your parent before getting married?"

8. Guest: "So, where are your parents?"

Response choices:

A. "Thank you for your consideration. However, I am confident that it will be fine."

B. "I assure you I have thought of that before; thank you, though."

C. I would prefer not to talk about that during this time."

D. "Unfortunately, not all of us have the same experiences with our parents."

E. "I am disappointed they will not be here as well. However, this is a choice they made."

F. "It is unfortunate that I am being blamed for my parents' choices, but this is a choice they made."

G. "I see you are trying to be kind and considerate of my feelings, but I assure you that I am not sad about this arrangement" or (ii) "I assure you that although I am sad about this arrangement, I have my supports in place if needed."

H. "I would like this special day to be just about those who have supported and loved us."

I.   "They will not be joining us today. Did you try the lobster?"

J.   "Yes, their behavior is disappointing. However, I am happy to be surrounded by those who support me on this special day."

Are there any other responses you'd like to add?

Maybe you came up with some responses that make you feel more prepared. Or maybe you simply read through the scenarios just to get an overall idea of some to keep in your back pocket for whenever they're needed. I understand personally how an offhand comment or seemingly innocent statement or question can leave us scrambling for an explanation, only to feel embarrassed over how we reacted—or to think of the perfect response the next morning in the shower! I find it is empowering to have a selection of phrases ready to give people—statements that are assertive and firm. This can reduce some of the retraumatization we might feel during these moments. Moreover, being able to better handle what others may say can help to heal shame.

The Importance of Positive Self-Talk

Abandonment sent us the message that we are defective and flawed, and thus deserving of abandonment. Many of us have internalized that message, and it manifests in our lives as negative self-talk swimming around in our minds. For survivors of this trauma, negative self-talk can happen almost daily, varying only in amount and strength.

You may be wondering, *Do I really do this?* Often, negative self-talk is second nature, so you likely do it every day without noticing. Negative self-talk can look like self-doubt, fear of rejection, hypervigilance, perfectionism, avoidance, or even self-loathing and isolation. You may not recognize it as self-doubt when you think something like *I'm not sure if I can do this; I always mess things up.* Your fear of rejection might tell you *They probably don't want to hear my opinion.* Your hypervigilance may see someone being distant and assume *They must be mad at me.* Your perfectionism might say *If I do everything right, I'll be accepted.* The more extreme our self-loathing, isolation, and avoidance, the stronger the messages:

I'm fundamentally flawed.

"Sorry to be such a burden."

I'm helpless and hopeless.

Why let anyone get close when they always leave eventually?

The best first step to combating negative self-talk rooted in shame is positive self-talk, fostering a healthy sense of self-worth and emotional well-being. Over time, by challenging and reframing destructive messages of unworthiness with affirming and compassionate self-talk, you can counterbalance the internalized narratives ingrained during abandonment. This shift in self-talk breaks down shame and allows for the creation of new spaces to cultivate more compassionate and empowering self-views.

The next exercise is designed to help you begin recognizing and reframing any negative self-talk you engage in. Read the introduction and have a journal or notebook handy to follow any of the writing prompts.

Exercise: Recognizing and Reframing Negative Self-Talk

When we begin the process of healing, we may not even be aware of how often we speak negatively about ourselves, which is why creating awareness is the first step to unlearning and changing this behavior. First, we need to define when and where it happens. When are you most likely to engage in negative self-talk? Read through the following scenario and imagine yourself in a similar experience:

Think back to a time when you last found yourself engaging in negative self-talk. It could be the aftermath of making a mistake, either at work or in a social situation. Maybe you received negative feedback in class or from a supervisor. Perhaps you'd just had an argument with a friend or partner. Stuck in a thought loop, you replayed the conversation over and over in your head until, before you knew it, you ended up back in the pattern of negative self-talk.

Step 1

First, mentally check off the comments you are likely to say to yourself during these moments. Feel free to rewrite them if needed on a piece of paper, or just list the numbers, such as 1, 5, 6. If those listed do not accurately reflect the way you speak to yourself, jot some of your own in your journal or notebook.

1. *I'm so stupid! No wonder I have so few friends.*

2. *That was so silly. I'm so embarrassed about the things I say.*

3. *I am sure my boss will fire me. I just keep messing up.*

4. *I should never have gone back to graduate school. I just can't keep up.*

5. *Why did I share my poem at open mic night? It was poorly written and made me look dumb.*

6. *If they knew the real me, they wouldn't date me. I'm difficult to love.*

7. *I just don't deserve nice things.*

8. *I'm such an idiot for speaking up during the meeting. This is why I should just stay quiet.*

Step 2

Take a moment to reflect on these statements. Notice how they are shaming, victim-blaming messages.

Many of these negative statements are so automatic that you may not even realize you are saying them, so recognizing them can take practice. However, over time, you will learn to catch yourself when saying them and to actively replace them with more neutral statements with less victim-blaming and negativity.

In your journal or notebook, take a moment to rephrase any of the statements that you commonly say to yourself. Use these two examples as a guide:

Statement #1: *I'm so stupid! No wonder I have so few friends.*

Reframing statement: *I said something a bit silly that felt embarrassing, but this is a normal human experience. If someone judges me based on my imperfections, they are not being a good friend. I deserve someone who loves me for who I am.*

Statement #6: *If they knew the real me, they wouldn't date me. I'm difficult to love.*

Reframing statement: *I'm not perfect because none of us are. I'm working on improving myself every day to be a better partner and friend.*

In this chapter, we explored shame as one of the major results of being abandoned by a caregiver, especially if it happened at a young age. We explored some of the negative messages from society and how this can feel retraumatizing. We went over the importance of using positive self-talk to combat these negative feelings or experiences.

Next, we will discuss some of the ways abandonment comes up in relationships and creates unhealthy patterns in relationships.

I am safe. What happened was not my fault.
I did not deserve to be abandoned.

Part 2

Uncovering

and

Healing

CHAPTER 4

The Ways Abandonment Can Manifest in Adult Relationships

[W]hat I always wanted was a dad who would love me as I was—somebody who would say, "I just love you. You could do anything right now. I'd still love you with unconditional love."

—Britney Spears, *The Woman in Me*

Workers at the treatment center where Riley lived had started to grow concerned over her self-harming behavior, so they sent her to me for treatment for depression. It was immediately apparent that she had been hurt badly and was not easily trusting of others. There was no opening up; no connection.

"This isn't going to work," said the medical director at the shelter health clinic during one of our weekly treatment meetings. "She won't open up or take her medicine, and it's a liability."

"Give me a few more weeks, please," I begged them.

They gave me two.

Our sessions started with coloring pictures and painting. Riley was in her mid thirties, but these activities, which we might associate with child therapy, helped bridge the gap. We talked about random interests, like music or movies. Slowly, she started opening up, though still maintaining her shield.

Eventually, we made a breakthrough.

"I knew I was trans for years," she confided to me, "but I had to hide it all through high school. Then, when I turned seventeen, all my friends started making plans for prom, but the idea of wearing a tux made me nauseous. I couldn't hide anymore, but I knew my parents would never understand or accept me.

"So I left the house in a tux, but changed into a dress in my friend's car. We kept to the back of the gym in the shadows, and not too many people recognized me, but still, I had the best time." She paused to laugh. "It was great! I finally got to be myself."

As I listened, I began understanding so much of what she had not yet said—why she had spent the past year living in a shelter, away from any family or support.

Her family had found the dress later and asked all sorts of intrusive and embarrassing questions—too many. Then the rumors caught up with her. People who'd seen her at prom started to make comments, not knowing the damage their seemingly innocuous comments might cause.

Her parents kicked her out a week before graduation, and she had been living in and out of shelters and treatment programs ever since. Her depression, self-loathing, and low self-worth overwhelmed her: Self-harm was the only way she knew how to make it through the experience.

I could finally see why Riley struggled to get close to others, especially people like me, staff members, or others in authority positions; why she would stay so guarded; and even why she self-harmed. Her parents had abandoned her in her time of need; this taught her she was wrong and unlovable. Those who were supposed to love and care for her proved themselves unreliable and willing to abandon her.

Note: If you are experiencing thoughts of self-harm or suicidal thoughts, contact your local emergency support services or hotline: call **988** or visit 988lifeline.org.

If you are struggling with coming out as LGBTQ+, seek affirming and caring support. Some options are The Trevor Project, or LGBT Foundation - Coming Out.

When witnessing someone who is unhoused and self-harming, or engaging in similar self-destructive behaviors such as substance use, society is often quick to place blame. Rarely do we stop to consider the story behind such a person's life—what happened to them to get them to where they are now. The automatic societal inclination is usually to blame the person who's struggling; to blame Riley for her depression and self-harming rather than the parents who kicked a child—*their child*—out of her home.

Now we're going to look at how your experience of abandonment may show up for you as an adult. Your trauma is likely finding its way into your day-to-day life. Perhaps, like Riley, you find it difficult to trust. Or maybe you struggle to develop close relationships.

How Abandonment Affects Relationships and Friendships

When you were abandoned, your caregiver broke the parental contract of unconditional love. You needed unconditional love, and its absence disrupted the developmental pathways in your brain. This likely affected your stability, self-esteem, and ability to create and maintain adult relationships and meaningful connections. You may struggle to believe you deserve such relationships, and you may not have the tools to navigate them in healthy ways.

Parents who nurture and love their children teach them that other people will be, for the most part, genuine and safe. When parents reject their children, those children develop the mindset that others will hurt them. The circumstances of your abandonment can affect how this plays out for you as an adult. If it happened after something you did—coming out as gay, experiencing a legal issue, or making a mistake at school—you likely interpreted the abandonment as a rejection of who you are or the mistakes you have made. Thus you may believe you are inherently flawed, so you deserved to be abandoned. When the abandonment happened after something the parent or family did—such as a parent remarrying or choosing a new life, moving away, or another act on their part—you may interpret this as your being unimportant or unworthy of love.

Perhaps you experienced some combination of those scenarios—or something altogether different. No matter the reason, the outcome was traumatic, and it has probably affected your ability to relate to and connect with others. It's helpful to look at the two extremes of how this can manifest: (1) a desperate quest for connection, love, and relationships, and (2) a fear of getting too close. These are both very normal reactions to having been abandoned by those who were supposed to love and protect you.

A Desperate Quest for Love and Connection

It's very common to respond with withdrawal and isolation, as Riley had. Other survivors may find themselves feeling the opposite—desperate for the social connection they never got from their parent(s). Unlike Riley's reaction, you may have become addicted to the act of meeting someone new, falling in love, and the intense feeling of being needed and "chosen." Yet, as the newness wears off, developing more emotional intimacy can make you feel anxious, frustrated, or fearful of again being abandoned. Sometimes, survivors develop a combination of the two, vacillating between avoiding people and desperately seeking love. The attachment struggles of survivors of parental abandonment often fall into two extremes: jumping from relationship to relationship or avoiding relationships altogether. Both are attempts to repair the wound of abandonment and avoid it happening again.

For healthy individuals who grew up in nurturing, supportive families, social support would usually serve as a supplement or complement to their lives. This helps empower them to more easily recover from a difficult or traumatic relationship or conflict in a friendship. For someone with a healthy support system and development, this conflict does not feel as devastating and life-ending as it does to the survivor of abandonment, to whom having a relationship or not can feel like the difference between life and death.

"In extreme situations, if an infant does not get consistent, safe, stable, and nurturing care, the crucial capacity to form and maintain healthy relationships won't develop" (Perry 2021). Safety and security from a parent or caregivers are necessary for a child to develop interpersonal experiences, healthy awareness of others, and relationship skills. Without those experiences, survivors of abandonment may end up seeking it through others. Desperate for the core belonging, love, and support that feels crucial to their survival, they often turn to interpersonal and romantic relationships as stand-ins for the foundational love and support they never received as a child.

Have you ever felt desperate for that feeling of being chosen or loved? That desperation reflects your unmet needs and your attempt to heal the deep wound of abandonment by seeking out what you never got from your caregiver who left: reassurance of your value and worth.

Do you have a pattern of getting in and out of relationships, displaying unhealthy qualities because you have not yet healed? That cycle is an unconscious effort to prove your own worthiness of love and affection.

Fear of Getting Too Close

Maybe you fear getting close to people, worried that such closeness will bring only pain and suffering when they leave. This avoidance is a defense mechanism to protect you from the pain you experienced when you were abandoned.

Many survivors feel anxious or uncomfortable at the prospect of getting to know a new person because they worry that this new person will also reject them. Do you ever have thoughts like *I have to be on my best behavior because if this person gets to know the real (flawed) me, they will reject me?* You may never have seen these thoughts as connected to your abandonment, but being vulnerable and open may bring up uncomfortable feelings of previous times when such vulnerability was rejected. You may hesitate to ever share such deep parts of yourself again and worry over the possibility that others will inevitably abandon you. Your behaviors and interactions with others may reflect these negative inner beliefs.

Like many who have been abandoned, Riley developed a fear and mistrust of others. This response makes sense! Her brain was trying to protect her from further pain and suffering. As a result, she developed what mental health professionals often describe as *avoidant behavior* or *avoidant attachment*—disruptions and disorders in the pathways that allow them to form and maintain healthy interpersonal relationships. Riley learned to keep her distance from others to avoid the pain of being hurt and abandoned again, afraid that if anyone really got to know her, they would dislike, reject, or abandon her.

Discovering Our Relationship Patterns

Trauma can manifest not only in how we form attachments or our fears of attachment, but also in other dysfunctional patterns. To alleviate their ongoing fear that if they upset others, they'll be rejected, survivors may adopt traits of codependency and people-pleasing. According to Darlene Lancer, a licensed marriage and family therapist and expert on codependency, this pattern is a common response to fears of rejection and of being left alone. Survivors act on inner impulses based on their history, rather than the logic of a healthy brain. As they depend on the feeling that comes from people around them being calm and content, they make constant and persistent efforts to ensure that others are happy, even those who have no reason or desire to leave (Lancer 2014).

Like someone stranded for days in a desert, looking for food and water, anyone starved of their basic childhood needs for support, love, and affection will naturally grow desperate looking for it. We may not realize our desperation for love or connection or how it manifests, but we feel it, and it impacts our behavior. I know I didn't realize I was engaging in this behavior until I was able to look back during my healing journey, and then it felt like a curtain had been lifted. If you are noticing that same curtain being lifted, please know that you are on the right track. You are uncovering and developing awareness of unhealthy patterns, which is a major step in the healing journey.

Remember, dear reader, we are acknowledging the origins of these behaviors not to cause shame, but rather to recognize and understand that our lack of skills in navigating relationships, our avoidance of conflict, our ignoring of red flags, and our inability to trust are all manifestations of our abandonment. By empowering ourselves with this knowledge, we have a better chance of working toward replacing those unhealthy patterns with healthy ones.

Recognizing Unhealthy versus Healthy Relationship Patterns

Do you think you could recognize a healthy relationship if you saw one? If you answered some version of no and have also experienced parental abandonment, you're not alone. With their formative years lacking in unconditional, secure love, abandoned children can struggle for the rest of their lives to understand what an unhealthy or healthy relationship looks like. Often, they never had a healthy example.

A healthy relationship is like a sturdy bridge—built on a strong foundation of trust, communication, and mutual support. In such a space, both individuals can share, comfort, and express themselves freely in a healthy give-and-take. Support and communication flow naturally. Both partners feel seen, valued, and secure. They acknowledge and respect one another's needs and aim for the continued growth and well-being of the connection.

Healthy starts veering into the realm of *unhealthy* when a relationship exhibits patterns of control, manipulation, and neglect. With parental abandonment, our developmental patterns distort, leaving us to form unhealthy relationships—dangerous, broken-down bridges threatening to collapse under the weight of unmet needs and unaddressed issues, and in urgent need of repair. Support feels one-sided. You may strain to communicate. Unspoken resentments may create uncomfortable tension. Trust may feel thin or nonexistent.

Over time, just as even the strongest bridge needs maintenance, all healthy relationships require nurturing, attention, and care. In healthy relationships, that's a parent's job—to always be a parent who cares for, supports, and protects their children. In the case of a young person who was abandoned, their parents did not do that, putting the child in an unfair position. If their parent "gives up" and leaves, either emotionally or physically, this act reinforces the child's reactionary behaviors of shame and abandonment into adulthood. This sets the stage for unhealthy relationship development.

For some survivors, the fear of being abandoned and left alone can keep them staying in unhealthy relationships for much longer than they should. Recall how previously we discussed the desperation for love and support that many survivors feel, so they also feel the need to always be in a relationship; this can sometimes mean staying in unhealthy or even abusive relationships. For some of you, abandonment fears might manifest as desperation to fix unhealthy relationships, both so no one can "give up" on you again, but also because you may fear "giving up" on the other person and being the one who abandons. When you don't recognize such behavior as unhealthy, you might also compete for a partner's attention, reflecting your desperate—but futile—childhood efforts to compete for your parent's attention, only to be abandoned by them.

Unknowingly, most survivors often enter into these unhealthy relationships because the unhealthy situation feels familiar, and they subconsciously desire to "redo" their story. If you grew up trying to get your parent to notice you while living in the same household, or you spent days wondering why the one who left never returned to you or even contacted you, you already have experienced a disruption to the healthy parent-child dynamic.

In a healthy family, as children grow to be teenagers, older adolescents, or college age, parents commonly have to work for their attention. Children may find such efforts annoying at times, but this normal, healthy dynamic demonstrates that someone thinks of them and watches over them; it reminds them that their parents are in control, which makes them feel safe and protected. However, in an unhealthy or dysfunctional dynamic, the parents often fail to put in such effort to gain their child's attention, leaving the child well aware that they are unthought of and unwatched—and thus unable to develop a healthy understanding of relationships.

This sets the stage for a survivor's developing unhealthy relationships, desperately trying to fulfill those unmet needs. They end up feeling they need to bring value—beauty, looks, money, accomplishments—to the relationship because they feel they have no intrinsic value in and of themselves. They may grow up struggling to navigate conflict and, as a result, avoiding it.

Do you have a long history of avoiding conflict, or does conflict always seem to surround you? Do you find yourself unsure how to navigate these difficulties in relationships, be they romantic or platonic? Do you struggle to handle conflict in a healthy way? You may have grown up believing that conflict, differing opinions, or simply being who you are brought about your abandonment. It's only natural that, as an adult, you might still feel apprehension or anxiety around conflict.

Few people *like* conflict. Most find it uncomfortable to some degree. However, for survivors of abandonment, it can feel like the end of the world. In their minds, conflict signals rejection and abandonment, so naturally they react to it as a threat.

I find that survivors of abandonment generally react to conflict in one of three ways:

- **Avoiding it at all costs:** Parental abandonment often leaves children frightened that any disagreement could lead to abandonment, so they avoid conflict. To preserve an appearance of harmony and prevent the discomfort of confrontation, they may withhold their opinions or fail to express their needs.

- **Fighting to the extreme:** Just as a survivor's abandoned inner child may lead them to react out of defensiveness and anger, the survivor may feel an overwhelming compulsion to fight. They feel that their defensive stance protects them and their dignity from potential harm or being left behind. To others, this may look like an inability to yield or compromise, constant conflict with others, intense arguments, or a tendency to push people away. Some survivors may even resort to physical fighting. While this in no way excuses violence, knowing its likely source can help survivors develop self-awareness to change their propensity for violent behavior.

- **Seeming to handle it, but being a nervous, struggling emotional wreck inside:** While some survivors of abandonment may seem to handle conflict appropriately on the surface, underneath, they may harbor a constant undercurrent of anxiety and self-doubt. Afraid of being vulnerable, they may mask their internal struggles with a facade of strength. Such mental dissonance can hinder authentic emotional connection.

Another common unhealthy relationship pattern for abandonment survivors is ignoring or excusing relationship red flags. Combined, their fear of abandonment and being alone and their desperate quest to find love and be chosen can drive survivors to push aside their gut feelings about toxic or unhealthy partners. In his book *The Body Keeps the Score: Brain, Mind, and Body in the Healing of Trauma*, renowned trauma expert Bessel van der Kolk notes that trauma survivors "often become expert at ignoring their gut feelings and in numbing [their] awareness of what is played out inside. They learn to hide from their selves" (2014).

Finally, abandonment can impact a child's ability to trust others. Parental abandonment disrupts a child's foundational belief that those closest will remain steadfast in their love and commitment, and this permeates their adult relationships. As Dr. Jonice Webb, an expert on emotional neglect, describes it, many survivors end up living their lives "constantly on guard for the possibility of being abandoned again." She writes: "When your parent abandons you, he or she is violating your most basic human need, which is to have parents who value and enjoy you. If the one who is meant to love and care for you the most in this world leaves you, it becomes very difficult to believe that anyone and everyone who becomes important to you will not do the same" (2018).

After abandonment, you may have found yourself living in a state of perpetual vigilance and hyperawareness for the looming possibility of being abandoned. This may keep you feeling guarded, unwilling to fully open up emotionally, and erecting emotional walls as a defense mechanism to shield yourself from potential abandonment.

How Abandonment Manifests in the Professional World

You may be wondering, *What does my abandonment have to do with my job?* It has a *lot* to do with it. Being abandoned by a parent affects our very sense of who we are, where we belong in the world, and how we relate to others, in personal *and* professional settings. It can manifest in our careers and professional spaces.

A constant thought loop telling us *If they really knew me and how I am, they would not like me* can make us feel like we always have to act in certain ways or put on a "professional" face. This entails more than simply using professional language in front of supervisors and in emails, or simply acting polite; rather, it's an overall sense that we need to completely change *who we are.* Many of my clients report the urge to take on a false self or persona in their professional roles or in public. Instead of being open and honest about our struggles, we might overcompensate by displaying perfection and rigidity in everything we do, so as to never be taken advantage of again. This defense mechanism against fears of abandonment keeps us from being vulnerable and open in professional relationships and friendships.

Our inner belief that we are defective and wrong may also cause us to struggle with criticism or feedback. Out of fear of letting others down, we may worry that unless we are valued or loved at work, we have no value as an employee. Many survivors grapple with an incessant need to achieve perfection, believing that if they are perfect in their job, they will be needed, and therefore much less likely to be left (passed over, sidelined, or let go). Being valuable becomes almost like a means of self-preservation—their way to protect or shield themselves against the abandonment they fear.

Our individual roles as community members can mimic these same traits. Community roles such as a position on the school PTA or at a place of worship are similar to professional roles and can bring out the same feelings: needing to be invaluable, struggling with feedback, and other coping behaviors that arise after abandonment.

Coping While Trying to Be a Good Parent

If you're a parent now yourself, you may struggle in your own parenting. This is common for many survivors, for reasons similar to those just discussed.

If you can relate to this, you may be struggling with the following:

- **Worrying about repeating the cycle:** You may know in your heart that you could never abandon your child, but you worry that what happened to you will cause the same disruptions to your family dynamics.

- **Difficulties with emotional regulation:** Abandonment has always made it hard for you to regulate difficult emotions, but now, faced with the stress of parenting, you may react in inappropriate ways. In addition to struggling to cope with your own feelings, you might also struggle with your children's feelings and emotions.

- **Overcompensating for what you didn't receive:** Never having received unconditional love and support, you may become overbearing in your love for your children, almost to the point of smothering them emotionally.

- **Struggles with codependency due to the way your abandonment manifests:** You may worry about allowing your children to experience negative feelings, arising from your own fears that accompany these feelings. You may worry that if your children experience these feelings they won't be able to handle them safely.

- **Attachment issues:** A history of insecure attachments may make it challenging for you to form healthy, secure attachment bonds with your own children.

- **Difficulties with being an authority figure:** You may be uncomfortable with all the responsibility that comes with that position of authority. In response, you may have relaxed boundaries with your children, acting almost as a peer rather than a parent.

- **Trust issues:** You may struggle with being vulnerable with others, including your spouse and your children.

- **Parentification:** Being abandoned when you were young, you may never have experienced secure support from one or both of your parents. This may lead you to unconsciously cast one of your children in the role of a surrogate spouse or emotional caregiver.

- **Inconsistent discipline:** If you were abandoned as a child or during a vulnerable time in young adulthood, you may struggle to set limits on punishments for your children. When you never learn the healthy discipline that comes from unconditional love, you may fear all discipline.

- **Overprotective behaviors:** You may be overprotective of your children in the presence of authority figures, such as with teachers, community figures, or even when they are with their other parent.

Navigating parenthood as a survivor of parental abandonment can be challenging, but when we understand the ways these challenges can manifest in our adult lives, we can recognize them in ourselves and move toward growth and healing. Parents who are coping with their own attachment struggles can seek support and resources and learn to communicate openly and honestly with their children and foster more secure emotional bonds. By acknowledging and actively addressing these patterns, abandonment survivors can break the cycle.

· This next exercise will teach you tools to bring awareness to triggers and stressors that come up to help you move ahead on your healing journey.

Exercise: Stop and Think

By bringing awareness to the triggers we experience throughout our day, we can empower ourselves to learn healthier ways of reacting and coping with the feelings and sensations that come up. Survivors of parental abandonment can often find themselves reacting to perceived slights in extreme ways that feel uncomfortable. By taking a moment to examine them, we can gain insight into how our individual abandonment manifests.

First, recall an event, person, or situation that recently bothered you in an extreme way at the time, but in hindsight made you wonder why it got you so upset. This could have been a conversation with a friend or partner that turned into a disagreement, or some other stressful event. It could be a comment you overheard or an experience you shared with family or coworkers at a holiday get-together. Feel free to take a note or two about the event in your journal to jog your memory.

Next, think about what you were feeling during that event. What is the first sensation or emotion that comes to mind? For some, it may be tension, the urge to get up and leave, or a desire to argue or even get physical. Without thinking too much, jot down the first few feelings that come to mind.

Now take a moment to recall everything we've covered in this chapter: common results of abandonment, the ways that old abandonment wounds manifest later in life, and the defense mechanisms that may result. Reflect on what might have been happening for you and how it relates to your abandonment.

Armed with this knowledge, when a similar situation occurs again, you can now *stop and think* before reacting. Stopping and thinking, even if just for a moment, can gain you more insight into how your history can drive your feelings and experiences. This is not to say that those reactions are wrong or even out of place—if someone purposely steps on your toe, you have every reason to be upset and to react, and an extreme reaction is perfectly normal for someone dealing with the trauma of abandonment. This exercise is about identifying when you may react disproportionately to an event, developing greater awareness so you can heal.

In this section, we've covered the ways that abandonment can affect our ability to maintain healthy relationships and the different ways that abandonment can affect us as a friend, as a partner, and even as an employee. We went over unhealthy and healthy relationship qualities and also ways to cope with your own history while trying to break the cycle of trauma as you start or maintain your own family. We briefly explored some of the negative results of abandonment, including some of the feelings that may come up. In this next chapter, we will dig deeper into negative feelings that come up during the healing process, as well as ways to cope with them.

CHAPTER 5

Negative Feelings That Come Up During Healing

Unconditional love. Not many guys here know that kind of love. A lot of them grew up without any kind of love at all. That hurts a man. It breaks him. It breaks him in ways that no person should be broken.

— Anthony Ray Hinton, *The Sun Does Shine*

Shortly after Stephen was born, his parents divorced and his father remarried. At first, his biological mother was involved in his life, showing up at Little League games or school plays while he was in elementary school. Then, over time, she started to decrease contact—a full year passed before he saw her again, then two, then five years passed with no contact from his mother. After that last time, she never came back.

Meanwhile, Stephen was academically gifted, excelled in school, and went on to earn a PhD in history. Eventually, he got a position teaching at a university near his hometown. The plaques hung on his office walls were constant reminders of his many career achievements.

But Stephen suffered from his mother's rejection well into his adult life. Despite all of his professional accomplishments, he never felt successful, complete, or even happy. Her abandonment plagued his waking hours; he always felt like something was wrong or missing. He felt incomplete. It showed up in his relationship with his wife and in his work life; it was a constant nagging feeling.

In our sessions, he often named his intellect as his downfall.

"If I didn't know what happened to me," he was wont to lament,
"I might be happier. But I do; I know the details and the rejection. That's
the issue—I'm unable to escape from it."

No matter what awards or recognitions he earned, he always felt
that he was not good enough for the person who was supposed to love
him above all else.

Identifying and Coping with Negative Feelings

Like many survivors, Stephen was smart and successful. Despite his mother's abandonment, he had gone on to excel in his career. However, that does not mean that Stephen had escaped suffering all the negative feelings stemming from the abandonment, just as many other children in his situation suffer. I believe that many of us are driven to seek the recognition that we did not receive from the parent who abandoned us, hoping that professional and social recognitions may somehow fill the gap and heal the wound. Unfortunately, and probably unsurprisingly, this doesn't happen.

Survivors often report negative feelings associated with their experience of abandonment: an ever-present emptiness or sadness; the constant feeling of having been left, and an inability to shake it. Most will experience one or more of the broad range of negative feelings that commonly come up during abandonment and the healing process. The list of feelings and emotions that could arise in our particular journey is practically endless. You may experience feelings in extreme forms or less intensely—remember, each of us experiences these feelings differently.

The following section describes some common negative feelings that may manifest after the experience of abandonment. Remember that if you do not notice or feel one or more of these feelings, that is okay. There are no rules for feelings. They can come and go in no particular order and in both unexpected and predictable ways.

Have your journal or notebook ready as you go through this list, so you can take notes on any feelings that you connect with, as well as any thoughts or feelings that come up as you read through. Each category has some tips or tools at the end to assist you if you can relate to this feeling. If you feel that these tips are beneficial for you in navigating that particular feeling or experience, feel free to jot them down, or note the page number to come back to. We're going to look at:

- Sadness and depression

- Hypervigilance, worry, and anxiety

- Grief and loss

- Anger and resentment

- Jealousy

- Guilt

Sadness and Depression

We start the work of developing understanding and healing by uncovering these feelings, but this can often feel like we'll have to get worse—way worse—before we can get better. Sadness, low self-worth, and depression are some of the most common mental health symptoms that come up in the aftermath of a child's abandonment, sometimes becoming more pronounced in adulthood. Such negative feelings or mental health symptoms can also lie dormant for many years, especially if the survivor is self-medicating with food or substances.

If you notice feelings of sadness or depression, I implore you to treat yourself with understanding and grace. Your feelings are normal and are signs that you are validating your history.

For sporadic or generally manageable sadness, simply allow those feelings to come and acknowledge their presence. At the same time, engage in self-care: take a hot bath, treat yourself to a pedicure, or spend time with people who make you feel good. If such feelings come on hard, fast, and strong to the point of feeling scary or uncomfortable—especially if accompanied by any thoughts of self-harm or suicide—please seek the support of a licensed therapist. (There is also a 24/7 support hotline available at 988.) With professional support to help you understand these normal parts of the healing process—which are nothing to be ashamed of—you can navigate and work through these negative feelings.

Hypervigilance, Worry, and Anxiety

Our developing brain, even as we move from adolescence to young adulthood, does not yet equip us to handle life independently. When we are abandoned in our formative years by those on whom we should be able to depend for safety and stability, we're thrust into a world in which we are unprepared to live. Abandonment removes the ground from underneath us, leaving us feeling like we have no place to safely land. As a result, we grow up with a lifelong sense of unease, worry, or hypervigilance.

No wonder many of us struggle with anxiety or a constant feeling of impending doom. Many feel like we are waiting for the next big thing to happen; for the other shoe to drop. Even as I approach the end of the second decade of my healing journey, I still have these moments. I want you to know that this is normal, while also validating the discomfort that these feelings bring.

If you recognize these feelings as they come up, that is great! Again, recognizing your symptoms is one of the most crucial aspects of healing because then you can empower yourself to support yourself through these feelings. Here are some ways of navigating them as they come up:

- **Acknowledge:** Let feelings come up and acknowledge them. The simple act of saying to yourself *I'm feeling really anxious right now* can help decrease that feeling to some degree.

- **Notice:** Notice where you feel the anxiety in your body. Is your heart racing? Do you feel shortness of breath? Bringing your focus to where you feel your anxiety helps you develop greater self-awareness around the feeling so you can manage it.

- **Slow down:** When negative feelings come up, you may feel like you need to "push through" and stay busy to distract yourself. However, such attempts can actually make you feel worse in the long run. Instead, allow yourself time to slow down, literally and figuratively. If you are running errands or doing chores around the house, literally slow your body down and practice being mindful of the tasks you are doing. Notice the suds on the dishes you are washing, or the feeling of the day's weather as you walk from your car to the bank. The act of slowing down your mind and body can help you be more mindful of feelings when they come up and can empower you to decrease symptoms.

Grief and Loss

We often hear the word "grief" and think of death, but abandonment can also instill a strong and singular sense of grief for both the loss of a secure base and the absence of a caring parent we never had. The grief that survivors feel over abandonment is particularly rough because they are grieving someone who often is still alive. Particularly if your parents abandoned you for who you are—becoming pregnant, being part of the LGBTQ community, not partaking in the family's faith, or another aspect that made you "different"—this may have reinforced your self-perception of being defective and bad, compounding your feelings of grief.

Many survivors report feeling intense grief or loss as they allow themselves to acknowledge more about their abandonment experience. Such grief can also creep up at random times. During holidays, birthdays, or other important or sentimental times of the year, those feelings can become painful. Seeing friends and extended family at their own holiday celebrations can trigger our feelings of grief over what we never had and likely will never have. Such traditional gatherings may reinforce the sense of loss and isolation that survivors of abandonment already feel. Nostalgia and memories can create uncomfortable pangs of heartbreak. Grief and loss are so real, and so difficult, yet they're often a less-talked-about result of abandonment. Here are some ways of navigating grief as it comes up:

- **Plan:** Planning for events or times of the year that you know will evoke feelings of grief can help empower you to better handle them. If you know to expect feelings of sadness on holidays or around your birthday, allow yourself to take a personal day off from work, schedule alone time, or plan a special day with your loved ones.

- **Make adjustments:** When specific functions or events trigger negative feelings, allow yourself to make adjustments. If listening to Christmas music during the holiday season feels too triggering, put on headphones with your own choice of music, or if you have the choice, simply change the station. If you are feeling grief over your upcoming wedding because your father will not be there to walk you down the aisle, change the event to include your own traditions that replace or eliminate that part of the ceremony.

We know that not all grief can be planned for; here are some tips for working through grief that pops up unexpectedly:

- **Stop and acknowledge:** It's important to take note of what is happening and what you are feeling or experiencing when unexpected moments of grief (or any difficult feeling) come up. This could be simply saying out loud to yourself (or silently, if you are among others) that this feeling is difficult (*This is a difficult moment that is unexpected*) or even naming the event out loud ("It feels painful to learn that my dad remarried; this was an unfair way to find out").

- **Give yourself grace and compassion:** The best way to support yourself when difficult feelings arise is to show yourself compassion. This could be taking a moment to yourself in private to self-soothe, or engaging in the visual imagery of your shield of protection (from chapter 2), or bringing to mind your perfect protector (from chapter 3).

Anger and Resentment

Anger and resentment are so common for survivors, yet many struggle to identify these emotions due to the stigma that they are "bad." Furthermore, the act of abandonment often robs the survivor of the ability to show healthy anger toward the one who caused the pain. Let me assure you that feelings of anger and resentment after abandonment are not only normal and expected, but *okay to have*—and are often a healthy sign of healing. It can feel unfair to have to go through life without caring, supportive parents, something most people seem to take for granted. This naturally brings about a lot of anger and resentment. When channeled constructively, anger can fuel empowerment and help us to set boundaries. It can serve as a protective shield, warding off further harm and asserting our inherent worth and dignity. However, when we are feeling angry, it can be hard to understand the benefit of anger and how we can use it constructively.

Anger may come up when you face situations that remind you of the unfairness of your abandonment. Learning that your parent remarried and that everyone was invited except you. Hearing that your parent has moved on and created a new family. These are common examples of events that may trigger feelings of anger and resentment. They can also manifest when celebrating events like weddings or graduations, where the spot usually held by a parent is open and empty. A man whose mother bothers so little to know her son or his life that she never learns about the birth of her first grandchild; a new college grad who watches their peers scan the crowd for their parents, knowing their own will not be there—these situations open up survivors to uncomfortable questions and opinions that can make them feel resentful or angry during what should be their happiest moments.

Society tends to shame people for their anger, especially survivors of family trauma. Some of the victim-blaming messages we might hear include:

- "They're your parents. They were doing the best they could."

- "They were dealing with their own struggles."

- "It's time to move on."

And many, many others.

When you notice these feelings of anger or resentment, I want you to first commend yourself. Yes, you heard me right. It might seem weird, but recognizing the experience of anger in your healing journey from abandonment is a good thing and a very important part of your healing.

When survivors believe that their abandonment is their own fault, that they deserved it, they are less likely to feel anger or that they were wronged. But children who were abandoned *were* wronged, and it is okay—and expected—to feel angry about it. Arriving at the point of noticing such feelings means you are coming to value and honor yourself. You should acknowledge and commend yourself for this.

Next, notice and respond to this anger or resentment in a healthy way. While we all have the right to our feelings, and I do encourage feeling them, it is not okay to treat others badly during our moments of anger. Instead of turning that anger on others, spend time honoring yourself and those feelings in a healthy way. Try one of the following:

- Take a long walk or hike, or do some light stretching.

- Write about it in a journal.

- Discuss your feelings with a supportive person or therapist.

- Allow yourself to cry or scream privately.

Jealousy

Jealousy can creep up as a close cousin of anger and resentment. In my years of healing, I have spent a lot of time in therapy processing feelings of resentment and jealousy over others who got to have "normal" families with "normal dysfunction," and parents who could still show up for their children when needed. You didn't have that either, and it wasn't fair.

Many survivors report feelings of jealousy—an often-constant sense of *It's just not fair* that can leave them feeling defective, angry, and ashamed for even having such negative feelings. Getting stuck with anger, resentment, or jealousy as a result of someone else's abandoning us is already unfair to begin with. The mere thought of this injustice can trigger those same negative feelings to manifest. It can feel like a cycle that we didn't ask for and yet are stuck repeating.

When we witness our peers celebrating happy milestones with their families and their parents, their moms and dads offering love and support during stressful times, it is only natural that we would feel the injustice of never being able to have the same. Still, feeling such jealousy can cause a great deal of shame—so much so, in fact, that many survivors stay in denial about feeling it—an understandable and natural consequence of abandonment.

If you feel jealousy, first remind yourself that it is okay to feel this way. Next, repeat the following statements. Write these out in your journal if you want, following the model. Even if you just say them in your head, that's okay—wherever you are in the moment, give yourself some quick validation and support:

> *I feel jealous about/that* _____, *and I have a right to feel that way. I am going to show myself support to help work through it.*

Guilt

Guilt can weigh heavily on survivors, manifesting as feelings of responsibility for the abandonment or a sense of inadequacy for not being "enough" to prevent it. The fear of confronting this guilt head-on or the instinct to avoid it altogether can be powerful, leading survivors to suppress their emotions rather than confront them. Guilt can be a barrier, because feelings of guilt often stem from a belief that we are somehow responsible for the abandonment or the circumstances surrounding it. Survivors may carry a burden of guilt, believing they could have done something differently·to prevent the abandonment or to earn the love and acceptance of the absent parent. This self-blame can weigh heavily on us, perpetuating feelings of inadequacy and unworthiness, and hindering our ability to move forward.

Additionally, guilt can serve as a form of self-punishment, leading us to believe we don't deserve to heal or find happiness. If this happens to you, you may find that this particular feeling creates a self-perpetuating cycle of negative self-talk and self-sabotage, making it difficult for you to prioritize your own well-being and engage in self-care activities that are essential for healing. Guilt can act as a powerful barrier to seeking help and support from others. Many may feel ashamed or embarrassed to admit their feelings of guilt, fearing judgment or rejection from loved ones or mental health professionals. This reluctance to open up and seek assistance can postpone or prolong the healing process and exacerbate feelings of isolation and loneliness.

Here are some ways of navigating guilt as it comes up:

- **Acknowledge that this feeling doesn't belong to you**: Ultimately, it is important to understand that these feelings of guilt are not yours to own. Guilt does not mean that you are doing the wrong thing or that the situation is your fault. You likely learned to internalize what happened to you as being your fault, when it was not. This guilt is often a feeling left over from that response.

- **Remember that guilt does not necessitate a change or action on your part**: Remind yourself that experiencing guilt doesn't automatically mandate a change in your behavior or actions. Just because you feel guilty doesn't mean you're obligated to alter your course or do something differently.

Effects of Not Dealing with Negative Feelings

It can be easy to think we can just suppress our negative feelings or distract ourselves from them with work, food, exercise, sex, or substances, but ignoring negative feelings will not make them go away. When we stop distracting ourselves enough to check on them, we still find them within us, often even worse than before.

Unfortunately, not dealing with negative feelings can lead to mental health symptoms, or even physical symptoms or illness. If you experienced abandonment and were not given the space and care to process the resulting feelings, or if you were shamed or told you were wrong for expressing yourself, you likely went on to suppress these negative emotions. However, you probably discovered that suppressing these feelings did not make them go away.

Those suppressed feelings likely had a negative impact on your health. Masking or denying inward feelings can suppress the body's immune response, leaving it more susceptible to illness. Feeling the need to conceal or repress emotions for fear of society disapproving and punishing more overt forms of expression can cause stress-related psychological reactions (Patel and Patel 2019).

Constant emotional suppression requires effort, which, in the long term, can develop into physical and psychological damage later in life (Elsig 2022; Morris et. al 2016; Chapman et al. 2013). Some common results of not dealing with negative feelings can include:

- High blood pressure (Nwanaji-Enwerem et al. 2022)

- Stroke (Tello 2019)

- Alcohol and/or substance abuse, or other addictions (Maté 2022)

- Cancer and autoimmune illnesses (Maté 2022)

- Heart disease (Tello 2019)

- Worsening of skin conditions such as psoriasis (Rigas et al. 2019)

Suppression is not the solution to the lingering negative feelings left behind from abandonment, but there are ways to work through these negative feelings so they do not impact your health. The first step is to begin the process of acknowledging and becoming aware of your negative feelings and how and when they come up. This process can naturally feel uncomfortable or uneasy, but discomfort is a normal experience during the healing process. Even when we start to shed some of our uncomfortable symptoms—like anger, depression, or anxiety—after having them with us for such a long time, not having them as much can naturally cause a certain level of discomfort.

Such discomfort may come and go or get worse before it gets better. Or it may just ebb and flow, with some days better or worse than others. It takes time to become more comfortable with acknowledging and navigating negative feelings. Rather than trying to make changes over a weekend, look at the bigger-picture changes that you make in the course of a month, a season, or a year. It is not realistic to expect yourself to completely heal your mental health symptoms within one week, and such expectations can actually backfire.

Healing is gradual. Go slowly in your process of understanding and processing any changes you might experience as a result. When we allow healing to unfold slowly at our own pace, it may help our progress to be more steady. Aim to acknowledge, increase awareness, and then start to replace some of the negative behaviors with more positive coping skills.

Coping Skills: What They Are, How to Use Them

Many survivors struggle to cope with negative feelings and most likely employ what we call "coping skills"—approaches to dealing with these unpleasant emotions and sensations—even if they do not realize it. The following is a list of some healthy coping skills people might commonly use to navigate times of emotional discomfort. Read through it and make a note in your journal if you relate to any. Feel free to skip over the ones that sound boring or tedious or don't interest you. The blank spaces at the end are to encourage you to think of other healthy coping skills you might be able to add. Write them in the list you have created in your journal.

- Take time to yourself for quiet.

- Practice yoga or meditation.

- Enjoy time with animals.

- Do some gardening.

- Exercise.

- Hike or walk outside.

- Read or listen to a podcast.

- Write in your journal.

- Attend support groups or therapy.

- Seek support through faith or spirituality.

- _____

- _____

- _____

It is often assumed that coping skills are positive. However, anything that helps you get through a negative feeling or experience is a coping skill, even if it is unhealthy. Ideally, we can learn to navigate negative emotions with coping skills that contribute to our emotional well-being and foster positive growth, but most survivors fall into using one or two skills that can occasionally border on being unhealthy. Navigating the trauma of abandonment may cause you to turn to these unhealthy coping skills more often—using alcohol or substances, food, sex, or other risky behaviors—to deal with feelings of loneliness, isolation, fear, and hopelessness. When persistent negative consequences, worsened mental health, or strained relationships tend to follow our actions during negative emotions, these may be signs we're dealing with unhealthy coping skills.

Addictions and Other Negative Coping Skills

When you turned to familiar comforts to avoid painful feelings—gobbling down a bag of chips, drinking a glass of wine, or seeking out yet another partner for love and affection to fill the empty hole inside—whether or not you knew it when you took such actions, you were engaging in coping skills. While these are all normal actions from time to time, when you use them in excess to distract yourself, mental health clinicians call these "maladaptive coping skills," the kind that provide temporary relief, but can cause long-term damage.

If you have developed any of the maladaptive coping skills described in this book—compulsive eating, seeking external validation, using substances, or any others—I want you to first show yourself support for being so resourceful. It may be surprising to consider, but using food or substances to cope was actually a protective effort—you were faced with trauma, and the lack of support that accompanies it, and you used what was available to protect yourself in a bad situation and survive the pain. These coping strategies helped you get through some rough times! Without them, you might not be where you are today, right now, reading this book. Thank yourself for doing what you needed to do to survive.

Still, this does not mean that such coping skills are best for you in the long term. While they may have been valuable resources to get you through the experience of your abandonment, at a certain point, when you realize your coping skills are becoming unhealthy, you need to know what to do and when to seek more support.

As we learn about our histories and develop healthier ways to cope with negative feelings, we also have to work on decreasing the unhealthy ones.

Notice that I said *decreasing*, not stopping overnight. If you realize you have been coping with food or substances, for example, do not try or expect to quit these behaviors by the end of this chapter. Nor should you feel ashamed or that your healing is "not working" if these behaviors do not go away completely. You have likely been dependent on these coping skills for some time, and trying to eliminate them before you are ready can be dangerous. Here's why:

While our maladaptive coping skills might decrease as we start to heal, in times of stress, we may still fall back on what we know. If you have taught yourself to cope by using food or substances and you return to them, give yourself validation and credit: you were doing what you needed to do to survive a difficult situation, calling on the support you know, and being resourceful.

If you recognize that you have been using unhealthy coping skills to an extent that you feel unable to stop, please seek support. There is no shame in admitting that you need help. In fact, you should take your recognition of the problem as a further sign that you are honoring and valuing yourself.

For help navigating unhealthy coping skills that may have turned into addictions, look for the support of a therapist who is trauma-informed and has a background in the behavior with which you are struggling: substance use, unhealthy or unsafe sexual behaviors, or using food to cope, to name a few. When you look for a licensed professional in your area, focus on their personality and seek someone with whom you think you would feel most comfortable being yourself.

If you do not choose to seek support through therapy at this time, that is okay. There is no pressure to do so before you are ready. Healing is a personal journey, and each of us goes at our own pace.

Activity: Self-Care Coping Skills Calendar

This activity can help improve your coping skills by increasing your commitment to self-care. To start, make a list in your journal of the activities that you enjoy. Write what makes you feel valued, rested, smart, healthy, and happy.

Next, grab a planner or desk calendar. The calendar app on your phone can work, too, if you prefer. You may also choose to draw out a chart like the one shown here as a guide. (A template is available as a free tool at www. newharbinger.com/54964.)

Now fill in some activities that you enjoy. Ideally, you should aim to pencil in one smaller activity per day and one larger activity per week, but you may need to work around your own work or school schedule depending on the time you have available. It doesn't matter which days of the week you choose to complete which activities. Maybe you have Sunday and Monday off, so consider those days to schedule a longer activity—a movie with friends or a nice long bath. Fill in the rest of the days with "mini" self-care rituals, like making sure to eat lunch on a work day, making time to enjoy a cup of coffee alone before work, taking a daily walk, reading, or taking time for meditation.

Then, without judgment or penalty either way, try to commit to following through. Continue each week, making any notes about feelings or experiences that come up as you notice them.

Unresolved negative feelings around the experience of abandonment can negatively affect our mental and physical health, and survivors often develop some unhelpful coping skills to survive these feelings. Once you can learn to identify the negative feelings that come up as a result of your abandonment experience, you can start to explore potential healthier ways to cope. Find a coping skill that results in more positive emotions, and you can prevent your trauma from continuing to affect you negatively.

You may still need to deal with experiences of retraumatization, which we discuss in the next chapter, but if you know where and how to expect this, when it happens you can be prepared to engage those healthy coping skills you've learned.

CHAPTER 6

Triggers and Retraumatization: A Common Roadblock to Healing

She had that same dream as always. She was chasing the blue car as it drove away, calling out for her mother, but could never catch it.

—Asha Lemmie, *Fifty Words for Rain*

Natalie was twelve when she found the courage to tell her mother that she was being sexually abused by her stepfather. Instead of receiving support and love, she was challenged, ridiculed, and shamed. Her mother refused to believe her, instead telling her to "stop that nonsense."

Natalie stayed silent about her experience for another three years before sharing what had happened with a teacher. Then the teacher called Natalie's home and shared the information with her mother.

When Natalie returned from school, her mother was waiting and furious. She accused Natalie of trying to "break up" her marriage.

"It was the late sixties," Natalie shared, as if in explanation. She sank deeper into the couch in my office. "We didn't have the resources we have now. People didn't want to get involved in other people's families. I never expected that teacher would call, but I guess she did."

Her mother had already been divorced once, "and she was lucky to remarry as a single mom," Natalie commented—having already learned to make excuses for her trauma.

Natalie ended up leaving home at sixteen and was married a year later.

Decades later, she still lives with the effects of her experience, and her relationship with her mother was never repaired. Her mother had abandoned her in her time of need.

Natalie told me, "I thought I escaped all of this, but it keeps coming back to me. I think of all that I lost out on because my mother could not protect me—could not even believe me." She began to cry. "My childhood, my youth, my safety—I lost all of that."

She had finally sought therapy after the death of her husband pushed her into a well of grief. Although his death was expected, the sense of loss and abandonment triggered all of those feelings of being alone and abandoned.

Understanding Triggers During Your Healing Journey

Traumatized people chronically feel unsafe inside their bodies: The past is alive in the form of gnawing interior discomfort.

—Bessel van der Kolk, *The Body Keeps the Score*

Many people may hear the words "triggered" or "trigger warning" and think of something that resurfaces a traumatic experience and the negative feelings that arise from it. This word crops up often on social media, sometimes inappropriately, adding to a somewhat negative stigma. But despite the way its popular use has somewhat diluted the intended meaning, "triggered" is actually a common mental health term. It refers to the activation of emotions, mental health symptoms, or other traumatic reactions by a stimulus or event (I'll offer some examples shortly). Triggers can lead to retraumatization. Let's take a closer look, using Natalie as an example.

For most survivors, parental abandonment leaves wounds. They may feel mad at the parent who abandoned them, but the act of abandonment disallows the child the luxury of expressing such an emotion to the one who left them. When children hold themselves back from expressing their anger out of fear of losing their caregivers' love and support, they are forced to redirect that anger and sadness inward. With no parent to direct their anger at, they may blame themselves in order to cope. This is why survivors of parental abandonment may be more sensitive to feelings of rejection and have difficulty trusting others or developing intimate relationships—triggers come up unexpectedly, remind us of this traumatic experience, and activate a traumatic response. Like Natalie, whose story we related at the beginning of the chapter, you may have gone for years thinking that, although your experience was difficult, perhaps you had moved past it. Then, much like Natalie, you may have had an experience such as the death of a loved one or a breakup or divorce that made you feel alone and brought up all of those feelings of abandonment again. This is one example of being triggered— even if unintentional or unintended, the experience brought up the negative feelings again for you.

Healing will be a different journey for each of us, but being triggered is a common element, and safely navigating your response when triggers come up is an important tool to develop on the healing journey. Sometimes, triggers can happen out of the blue—hearing a familiar song playing at the grocery store, or hearing a voice that sounds like the parent who left. Triggers can be a scenario or scene, event, sight, sound, or even a specific time of year. Here are some examples of common triggers:

- Seeing a family eating out at a restaurant, noticing the parents speaking kindly to their children and each other, or just being happy together

- Messages from media during holidays that put emphasis on being with family, or images of people with both parents during holiday gatherings that reinforce what you do not have

- Conversations with friends and family who may intend to offer well-meaning support but end up using victim-blaming language or language that might indicate doubt in the survivor's description of their experience

- Discussions that violate your emotional boundaries or put you in situations where you may be forced to defend yourself, such as a friend insisting that you should reach out to the parent who abandoned you

- Seeing pictures of people with their parents or families on social media, reminding you of what you do not have

- Looking at old pictures of you and the parent who abandoned you, reminding you either of good times or that the good times were rare

- Seeing mutual family or friends post information about your parent who abandoned you, like information about a recent family gathering or holiday meal that they attended

- Weddings, birthdays, graduations, or other family celebrations

- Certain sounds or music: listening to certain genres or bands that remind you of a point in your life or of the person who left

- Specific food, as so much about culture and family is wrapped up in eating (a Fourth of July BBQ reminding you of when your dad used to grill for the family; eating homemade hummus or labneh reminding you of your mother's cooking before she left, when she used to make food representing her family heritage)

For many survivors of parental abandonment, talking about the events behind their abandonment or why their parents are not in their lives anymore can feel extremely stressful. Those who have not experienced parental abandonment will have a hard time understanding it, which means most of them will at some point offer hurtful questions or statements without realizing the impact of their words. When they show you pictures of their own families, or ask where a certain parent is during important events such as holidays, or urge you to "just call them—they're your mother/father," their well-meaning but still harmful statements can cause you to relive the negative emotions of your experience.

Someone's seemingly simple query—"Why aren't you going home for the holidays?"—can bring you right back to that feeling of being a child, alone, wondering why your parent has not come to see you. In this moment, the initial rush of feelings can often include the need to excuse or explain, as well as shame for being in such a position in the first place.

Some triggers are very personal and often specific to your experiences or background—seeing certain landmarks that you used to frequent as a family, or visiting an art gallery if your parent was an artist. There is no limit or criteria to the triggers that you might feel.

Whenever these triggering moments happen, try not to shame yourself. This is crucial. You are having a human reaction to a trauma you experienced that was neither your fault nor within your ability to prevent or stop. The key to managing triggers is not to ignore or even prevent them; it is knowing to expect them and empowering yourself with ways to respond when they happen.

Exercise: Coping with Triggers

Think back to the most recent time you felt triggered. It could have been while watching a movie about a parent abandoning a child, or even about a parent who loves their child. Maybe it was a familiar smell, like pine reminding you of winters during your childhood and cutting down the family Christmas tree. It's okay if you can't remember specifics. Often, forgetting specific events or feelings we experienced during stressful moments is our brain's way of moving on.

Have your journal handy as you go through this list. Be open to whatever comes up in your mind as you attempt to revisit that stressful moment. Follow the steps as you reexperience this feeling in practice for when these moments come up in real life:

1. **Validate:** Validating your feelings is a critical first step. No matter where you are, give yourself a moment of validation. This can be as simple as something like *This is a triggering moment for me* or *It's hard for me to see/hear that.* If you are alone at home or in your car, it may help to say it out loud. If you are in a public place, speaking silently inside your head is fine.

2. **Give yourself support:** Keep it simple. Tell yourself *You're having a normal reaction, This is okay,* or *I didn't deserve what happened to me.* Go slowly for the next few minutes or hours until the feeling has passed.

3. **Get curious:** Ask yourself: *What is this trigger trying to show me?* For some, the answer may come immediately: *It is hard for me to hear this song because my mom used to play it on the record player and it reminds me of happy times;* or *Watching a father walk his daughter down the aisle at her wedding is difficult for me, even when in a movie, because it reminds me of what I missed out on.*

4. **Figure out what you need to move forward:** Validation is often enough for some people to move forward, but there is no right or wrong answer. Do you need to spend a couple of minutes in your office before going back out to work? Do you need to take a few minutes to look at cute kitten pictures or funny videos on social media? Allow yourself the time to do whatever you need to, to be able to move forward.

Triggers are a normal part of the healing process. So normal, in fact, that we should expect them. For each individual, those triggers will be different, but the more we dig into our negative emotions and healthy ways to cope, the better prepared we can be to navigate them. Even those who have spent years working on their healing may find themselves triggered. Now, when you find yourself experiencing these or other triggers, you know to recognize these as triggers and do your best to use these steps when they happen. While the triggering events may not go away, over time, we become more equipped to manage our way through them.

When Triggers Lead to Retraumatization

Healing from trauma does not mean we never again experience negative feelings; rather, we learn ways to cope that allow us to better live in harmony with them. Through mindful awareness rather than trigger responses and unhealthy, hyperreactive survival strategies, we can learn to adapt, to be better prepared to ride the waves of negative feelings that come up during healing.

Retraumatization is a living representation of a harrowing experience from the past, and there are many ways that a survivor of parental abandonment might be reminded of that experience. Certain situations or triggers transport our mind and body back in time to relive that past traumatic experience. While triggers are a reminder of our past traumas, retraumatization happens when we reexperience the original trauma. With retraumatization, there is often a trigger, as well as a now negative association with the new, now traumatic event. One common trigger is hearing a familiar song, whereas a common example of retraumatization might be when someone experiences abandonment again: either by a partner or another parent, or after being rejected again by the parent who abandoned you.

Retraumatization happens when stressors in a survivor's environment— the smell, the lighting, the space itself, or even a new relationship that mimics a traumatic one—actually cause them to reexperience a previous traumatic event, though they may not always realize what they are experiencing or why.

According to the Substance Abuse and Mental Health Services Administration (SAMHSA), some other symptoms of retraumatization can include:

- Flashbacks and nightmares

- Negative thoughts, anxiousness, or fear

- Trouble sleeping and/or staying focused

- Fatigue or low energy

- Social isolation and avoidance

- Intense negative emotions

- Inability to control emotions

- Strong physical reactions to triggers—fast breathing, rapid heartbeat, increased perspiration, and so on

A Common Retraumatization: When They Get a New Family

For some survivors, the parent who abandons them goes on to enter a new family. They may learn this at the time, when that parent tells them they are leaving to start a new family, or they may learn about it only years after the abandonment happened, through searching for the parent on social media or hearing about it from mutual friends or connections. When I found out from extended family that my father had remarried, and that I was never invited or involved, it devastated me. Having this knowledge compounded the abandonment I already felt and further retraumatized me—a scenario that happens every day to survivors learning of a parent's new marriage, or even babies or children from a new relationship.

Separation and divorce are normal parts of life that can and should be handled in a healthy way. People end relationships every day without cutting ties with their children. In fact, when parents split up in a way that prioritizes the mental health and support of their children and allows for healthy co-parenting, children observe this and learn how to manage and navigate conflict and relationships.

However, emotionally immature adults who are unable to manage this in a healthy way are often involved in toxic, high-conflict splits that put their children in the middle. A parent willing to justify abandoning their child would likely also remarry after splitting without any regard for or acknowledgment of the children's feelings about it or the devastating effects it might have. However it happens, and no matter the child's age, the experience of having a parent start a new family can feel retraumatizing for the child that the parent abandoned, reinforcing the message to their child that they do not matter to their parent.

As you go through your life, you will likely—indeed, undoubtedly—face reminders of these repeated experiences of rejection by a parent and the negative feelings that come up as a result. Without a supportive environment to help navigate this, you may have used maladaptive coping skills to survive those triggers and periods of retraumatization. If you encounter such moments, remind yourself that your reaction to triggering experiences is normal, based on your history of abandonment. Be self-supportive, validate your feelings, and go at your own pace to get through them in more positive ways.

By exploring some of the ways retraumatization can happen, including when we reach out to a parent and get rejected or blamed, we can learn to acknowledge and validate the feelings that follow. In the same way, all of the unique ways people may experience grief as the result of their parental abandonment are normal and allowed, and our first, best step in navigating them is to acknowledge and validate them. The following activity will help to organize and channel some of these feelings as they come up during your journey.

Activity: Letter to Them

It can be difficult to articulate the many feelings that come up when we experience abandonment, even more so when we are retraumatized during this experience. The feelings come so intensely, and they may even be conflicting or confusing. This activity can help with this process, but make sure to complete it when you are alone and have some privacy—ideally at the end of the day, or on a day when you have nowhere to be.

Completing this activity will likely bring up some negative feelings. If they are already present, they will likely get worse. Remember, this is okay.

It is part of the experience of healing, and you now have gained more tools to help you work through them. We reviewed coping skills prior to this activity, so you will have several fresh in your mind to choose from.

Your objective is to write a letter to the person who abandoned you, but with a twist: Write the letter with your nondominant hand. This common therapeutic technique is used to channel the client's inner child. The act of writing with our nondominant hand is reminiscent of childhood when we are learning to write. It is also a symbolic beginning for the process of learning about ourselves and the world around us.

Get your journal ready and grab any writing instrument—ideally one that is comfortable to write with, such as a pen or marker, but anything that can create letters will work. If you are ambidextrous, choose the hand you write with less often. This activity is best completed on paper rather than a computer—it can be lined, unlined, or just a random piece of scrap paper. Avoid thinking about handwriting, grammar, punctuation, or other rules of writing—these could distract you from your purpose of getting the feelings out. A wide-tip marker, crayon, or anything else less refined than a precise point can help you avoid focusing on grammar and sentence structure, but you can use whatever you have available.

Set the timer for two to three minutes; you can extend this time if the timer goes off and you want to keep writing! Then, using the following prompt, start writing:

Dear _____ [parent who abandoned you]

When you abandoned me, I _____

Post-Activity Support

When you are done—either when the timer goes off or when you feel you have said everything you had inside you—take a moment and breathe. Many people start crying as they write. This is normal. Allow the tears to come for as long as you need to. Remember your perfect protector from an earlier chapter and recall them if needed. Take a hot bath or shower, then put on some comfortable clothes.

Check in with yourself every fifteen minutes or so, taking note of the feelings you experience and where you feel them in your body. What do you need? Take some time to prepare a hot cup of tea or a snack. Call or text a friend. Take whatever additional support you need for the remainder of the day or evening. If you feel that this activity brings up feelings that are unmanageable, please seek the support of a licensed mental health professional.

We have reached the end of part 2 and the beginning of part 3, "Moving Forward," where we'll discuss ways to increase empowerment and move forward with healing. As you continue to read, remember that you have the tools to heal. Also remember that healing is not linear; it is much more like a wave that ebbs and flows. Finishing a specific chapter or section that talks about negative feelings does not mean that those feelings will no longer affect you; rather, this means you have grown in your awareness and your ability to respond and are continuing on your journey to healing.

Affirmations: I am healing.
I am worth loving.
I am a good person.

Part 3

Moving

Forward

CHAPTER 7

Increasing Empowerment to Improve Healing

The greatest sources of our suffering are the lies we tell ourselves.
—Bessel A. van der Kolk

Brian's mother had struggled with mental illness her whole life. She tried and failed with different medications that never seemed to work, eventually self-medicating with alcohol to help stabilize some of her symptoms. This, of course, led to other problems, including her leaving Brian alone for days on end, until he eventually left on his own at age nineteen.

A couple of years after he left, his mother was court ordered to an alcohol rehab treatment center. She got sober and started working with a psychiatrist who helped her find the right combination of medications to help her live a fulfilling life. Many years later, Brian's little sister, Elisa, was born.

As Elisa grew up, her mother was attentive, loving, stable, and most important, sober. Brian, on the other hand, no longer knew his mother at all. As adults, he and Elisa grappled with a strained sibling relationship. Brian had had a parent who struggled with substance use and other demons, who abandoned him; he considered his aunt his caregiver. He felt resentful that his sister had gotten their mother's "good side" and Elisa was unable to understand his experience. Despite what they shared, they had ended up very different from each other.

Family Dynamics: Abandonment Affects the Whole Family

Family dynamics are inherently complex, and abandonment compounds those challenges. When parents physically abandon their children—leave them, kick them out, or move away and out of their lives—or emotionally abandon them due to mental health conditions, substance use, or other intentional or unintentional causes, the experience impacts multiple relationships. Children are not responsible for their parents' decisions, but experiences of abandonment, neglect, and other forms of dysfunction or abuse can create unfair divisions among siblings.

As with Brian and Elisa, these situations can lead to resentment and conflict, as each sibling grapples with the unfairness of their shared experiences. Survivors of parental abandonment may grow up with little to no meaningful connections with siblings or extended family; they may even endure profound isolation within their familial network. Their siblings may experience a mix of confusion, guilt, and resentment toward both the abandoned child and their parents who abandoned them. They may feel neglected or overshadowed by the crisis and struggle to understand the disruption to their family dynamics.

Many of my clients report resentful feelings toward siblings who never experienced abandonment, but some say their siblings express resentment toward *them* for what they interpret as being "put in the middle." As I often reiterate, this unfairly places the blame on the victim of abandonment, but such victim-blaming thinking is unfortunately common. When people make remarks like, "Well, Dad and Emily never got along anyway," they blame the survivor along with the one who abandoned them, without recognizing the abandonment. When this message reaches Emily's niece, cousins, and other family members, it perpetuates that indictment of blame.

Abandonment ripples through the entire family structure, leaving no member untouched. Siblings, cousins, aunts, uncles, and extended family—everyone's role has to shift to make way for this new arrangement. Some may become enablers, like an aunt or uncle reinforcing the behavior of the parent who left. Some may also be victims. As my client Tiffany put it, "I know my brother's abandonment by our mother was not his fault, but I worried that if I 'stuck up' for him then I would be next." Parental abandonment puts other vulnerable family members, particularly younger ones, in unfair positions, navigating unfamiliar territory where they feel uncomfortable and in the middle.

Coping When Siblings Had a Different Relationship

When a child realizes their sibling had a different relationship with the parent who abandoned them, it can generate complex emotions, including feelings of sadness, anger, jealousy, or even resentment. It can feel invalidating and isolating, and it reinforces your feelings of low self-worth and self-blame. It can be easy to believe that their inability to be the parent you needed was actually your fault when it turned out they could be that parent for your siblings.

One client said about his abandonment, "I feel like any time I mention it, I'm invalidating my brother's experience with our father."

"It seems like my sister will always be in the middle," said another.

Such sentiments are common. Survivors often report feeling guilty about these very real and valid feelings, and coping with them can be challenging. If your experience was in any way similar, try to show yourself empathy and understanding.

First, acknowledge and validate your feelings. Allow yourself to feel these emotions without judgment, and recognize them as a natural response to an unfair situation—because experiencing parental abandonment is indeed unfair. I hope at this point you have notes in your journal to quickly reference tips from previous exercises that can help soothe these feelings.

Though it may feel hard to resist, try to avoid comparing experiences or resenting your sibling for their relationship with the parent who abandoned you. Instead, try to have open, honest conversations with that sibling about your feelings and experiences, to foster understanding and strengthen your relationship. Communication is key. The following activity will help you practice initiating this conversation in an open, nonconfrontational way.

Activity: Communication Techniques— Role-Play Prompts

Here are some tips to navigate difficult conversations around your abandonment with siblings. As you read through, make notes in your journal of ideas or things you could say. Some may choose to practice out loud with a trusted friend, therapist, coach, or partner.

- **Determine their receptiveness to this conversation:** Some siblings may not be able to participate if they are struggling with mental health or substance use. Others may have made it clear, through words or actions, that their alliance is with your parent and not you. As much as it hurts to realize, having such a sensitive conversation with someone who is not receptive may end up worsening the relationship in the long run. If you think they may be receptive, however, read on for the next steps.

- **Choose the right time and place:** Find a quiet, private space where you can have an open and honest conversation without distractions or interruptions. Pick a time when both you and your siblings are calm and emotionally prepared to discuss the topic.

- **Approach with empathy and understanding:** Empathy, understanding, and patience can foster healing conversations that strengthen relationships and work toward reconciliation, but admittedly it can be difficult to show empathy for those whose life seemed better or easier without the abandonment you experienced. As children, we are all products of our parents' choices. Acknowledging this can help remind you where the responsibility for what happened lies—with the adult, your parent—so you can better navigate feelings of resentment or injustice with other family members. Each sibling will have their own perspective and emotional response to the abandonment. Acknowledge their feelings and experiences without judgment or blame, and reflect on the ways they might also be a victim of a parent's decision to abandon their child to help generate empathy.

- **Use "I" statements:** Express your feelings and experiences from your own perspective by using "I" statements to avoid defensiveness and encourage open communication. For example, rather than "You pushed me aside," say "I felt pushed aside when . . ."

- **Listen actively:** Give your siblings the opportunity to express their thoughts and feelings without interruption. Show empathy and validation by acknowledging their emotions and experiences, even if they differ from yours.

- **Remember, they are not to blame:** Your parent or caregiver put you and your siblings in this situation. It's challenging, especially if you feel they had it easier because they were not abandoned, but remember, your siblings did not make that decision.

- **Practice self-care:** During these conversations with your siblings, remember to prioritize self-care throughout the process. Take breaks when needed. Engage in activities that bring you comfort and joy and promote emotional well-being, such as exercise, mindfulness, creative expression, or spending time in nature.

- **Seek support if needed:** If conversations become too difficult or emotionally overwhelming, consider seeking support from a therapist or counselor who can help facilitate communication and provide guidance in navigating family dynamics.

As you navigate these conversations and feelings about siblings and the parent who left, remember, you do not have to go through your journey of healing and self-discovery alone. Seek out trusted friends or family members, mentors, or support groups to build a network outside of the dysfunctional dynamic for validation, empathy, guidance, and additional resources. For many survivors of family and parental abandonment, a "chosen family" can provide that support.

Chosen Family: An Important Support Resource for Survivors

Support is essential, not only for trauma recovery but also for overall emotional well-being. Research consistently shows that social support is associated with better physical health outcomes (Taylor 2011). Strong social connections reduce the risk of chronic diseases, boost immune function, and promote faster recovery from illness or injury. Social isolation and loneliness, on the other hand, are linked to adverse health effects, including increased mortality risk (Wang et al. 2023).

A chosen family is a supportive network of individuals who provide love, acceptance, and companionship in the absence of biological family ties. Chosen family members may include friends, mentors, partners, or other trusted figures who offer emotional support, stability, and a sense of belonging. Social support may not be exactly the same as a supportive parent or caregiver, but many survivors of dysfunctional environments, like those that result from parental abandonment, will create a chosen family to replace what they never received in parental support. Their chosen families are often instrumental in helping them cope with stress and the emotional fallout of abandonment, providing a safe space to process feelings of loss, rejection, and betrayal, and to tap into much-needed empathy and encouragement. By offering unconditional love and solidarity to fill the void left by parental absence, a chosen family serves as a source of resilience and healing.

Finding a chosen family support system can be a meaningful and empowering process. If you already have your chosen family, I am so happy for you! This is an advantage for your healing. Many other survivors still lack this essential support, especially in today's age of digital networking and increased screen time, when meeting new people can seem difficult. If you relate to this challenge, here are some tips for finding and nurturing these important connections:

- **Identify shared values**: Look for individuals who share your values, beliefs, and interests to form a foundation for strong connections that provide a sense of belonging and understanding.

- **Seek out supportive spaces:** Explore communities, organizations, or social groups where you feel accepted and supported. This could include LGBTQ+ groups, hobby clubs, religious or spiritual communities, or online forums dedicated to specific interests or identities.

- **Nurture existing relationships:** Invest time and effort in cultivating deeper connections and mutual trust with friends, colleagues, or acquaintances who demonstrate empathy, acceptance, and reliability.

- **Be open to new connections:** Attend social events, workshops, or gatherings where people are more likely to share your values and interests, and stay open to the idea of welcoming new people into your chosen family.

- **Communicate your needs:** Be honest and open about your boundaries, expectations, and preferences for potential chosen family members to ensure that those relationships are built on mutual understanding and respect.

- **Practice self-care and self-compassion:** As you navigate the process of creating a chosen family, remember your own well-being. Building meaningful relationships takes time and effort; be patient and understanding with yourself. Prioritize activities that bring you joy and fulfillment.

Boundaries: An Essential Aspect of Healing

We have already mentioned the idea of setting boundaries on the healing journey, including when we're having difficult conversations with siblings and other family members. But what are boundaries? They are invisible guidelines—physical, spiritual, emotional, psychological, financial, and so on—that we establish between ourselves and others. These define our own needs and preferences and the limits set on behaviors we consider appropriate and acceptable, for ourselves and others. By clearly defining and communicating healthy boundaries, we foster healthy and respectful interactions, free from manipulation, people-pleasing, or self-neglect, and we cultivate healthier relationships.

Healthy boundaries can provide survivors with a sense of agency, self-respect, and protection from retraumatization throughout their healing journey. But many survivors of family trauma, especially from abandonment, were not taught healthy boundaries. When their parents abandon them during their time of need, children interpret this as their needs and boundaries being unimportant, and potentially even a burden or annoyance to others. Many survivors have to learn to reestablish their boundaries, often starting from square one: identifying what their boundaries even are and, more importantly, how to implement them.

Activity: Identifying and Establishing Boundaries

Only you can determine your own boundaries. But, like many survivors, you may struggle to identify those boundaries or know where to start looking for them. This is normal. Read through the following tips to help you work through this process with your journal handy to take note of anything that comes up for you:

- **Write down your values and needs:** Reflect on your beliefs and needs, considering what you value in your relationships, work, and personal space. This may be practicing your faith; having time with children or pets, or time to yourself; or preparing healthy meals, to name a few. Jot down whatever comes to mind.

- **Notice your emotions:** Do you tense up when someone cuts in front of you in line? Do your eyes well up with tears when someone asks about your weight? Our emotions often tell us a lot about our boundaries, so pay attention to your emotional responses and physical sensations in different situations. Reflect on past experiences when you felt uncomfortable, stressed, or overwhelmed, as these can be signs that your boundaries are being crossed or violated. Use these experiences as learning opportunities to better understand your own boundaries and preferences.

- **Identify your limits**: Think about what you are willing and unwilling to tolerate in your interactions with others. Consider your emotional, physical, and mental limits, and be honest with yourself about what you need to feel safe and respected. Are conversations about your body or relationship off-limits? Are you bothered when someone talks about their political views? These might be possible boundaries for you. Remember, there is no right answer. We each have our own boundaries. If something does not feel right, that is all the permission you need to have this be a boundary for you.

- **Practice implementing**: Starting small is key. When you're first establishing and implementing boundaries, starting small will help minimize discomfort. One client of mine was so afraid to shut off her notifications and take time for herself that she kept her phone at full volume, twenty-four hours a day. Her sisters often leaned on her for emotional and financial support, reaching out for it even in the middle of the night. When she first identified this as a potential boundary for her, she felt terribly guilty about turning off her phone, so we started small—just turning down the volume. Soon, she was able to turn off the phone between midnight and 6 a.m. Today, she keeps her phone on silent while she sleeps, without feeling guilt or worry.

- **Acknowledge discomfort while recognizing that it does not require you to take action or change**: As you identify and implement boundaries, many feelings may come up. When you first stand up for yourself, it may feel uncomfortable. You might wonder *Was that mean of me? Are they mad?* or similar thoughts.

Recognize and acknowledge that these feelings are okay, but remember: *Just because you feel discomfort does not mean you are doing anything wrong!* It is okay to say, "I feel guilty refusing to help my sister pay for her wedding because I wish I could help," while also recognizing that this is a boundary and the best decision for you and your family.

Now that we have discussed some of the ways abandonment affects the whole family, including relationships with siblings, and some of the ways to handle and navigate this, we can dig deeper into the healing part of your journey. Next, we will explore forgiveness and whether or not it is appropriate to your situation, as well as reconciliation and the mixed feelings that topic brings, and any grief that may come from those experiences. As we get down to the last couple of chapters, you may feel tempted to just push through, but it's important to take your time; these discussions can create difficult and unpredictable feelings. As always, take time to remember self-care, keep your journal or notebook nearby while reading, and read and digest the information slowly.

CHAPTER 8

Healing Does Not Mean Forgetting

Whether we realize it or not, it is our woundedness, or how we cope with it, that dictates much of our behavior, shapes our social habits, and informs our ways of thinking about the world.

—Gabor Maté, *The Myth of Normal: Trauma, Illness, and Healing in a Toxic Culture*

From as early as she can remember, Carinne felt that her mother was bothered by her. She was born with many medical concerns, and her mother, who thought that caring for her was "too much," hired a nanny to do it instead.

Carinne grew up in an affluent neighborhood and always had everything she needed physically—food, school supplies, and the best medical support money could buy—so, few would think to feel bad for her. The school never flagged her as someone with whom the social worker needed to check in.

Still, she always felt that yearning, like a hole that remained unfilled.

In one session, she cried, "I needed a mother, not a newer, more high-tech wheelchair!"

Her disability kept Carinne at home into adulthood, but although they lived in the same house, her mother barely acknowledged or interacted with her. Her mother abandoned her while living in the same household.

After spending over four decades being shunned by a caregiver who was like a stranger to her, Carinne came to me to deal with feelings of depression that manifested as anger. Her primary care doctor had prescribed an antidepressant, but, unsurprisingly, it didn't work. Her mother was in her late seventies and in cognitive decline, barely remembering who her daughter was and often perceiving Carinne to be her late sister. Not only was Carinne struggling with the pain of rejection and abandonment of her mother, but she was losing her mother again due to her cognitive decline.

In our first session, she asked, "How can I move forward knowing my mother will never—can never—acknowledge what she did to me?"

How to Move Forward Without Acknowledgment

Like many people who were abandoned by a parent, Carinne grew up with feelings of resentment and sadness, but her mother would never be able to acknowledge the wrongdoing of abandoning her. Many of my clients express a similarly harsh reality: Closure from the absent parent or caregiver may never come. For some, it's because they have passed or declined medically or cognitively to the point of incapacity; for others, the absent parent simply refuses to acknowledge their actions. Regardless of the reason, the lack of acknowledgment can deepen the wounds of abandonment and intensify feelings of rejection and unworthiness.

We may never receive the validation or apology we crave from our absent parent, and grappling with this painful reality often involves both grieving what we lost or never had, as well as creating room for self-healing and acceptance. Rather than condoning the abandonment or minimizing its impact, acceptance is about freeing yourself from the constant yearning for acknowledgment that may never materialize, which can keep you from healing.

In this part of the book, we will work on reframing the narrative from one of victimhood to one of resilience and empowerment. You will learn to find closure within yourself and define your worth and identity independent of your parent's actions or lack thereof. We will continue to discuss ways to nurture supportive relationships and build a chosen family for the love, acceptance, and validation that may be missing from the absent parent. Survivors can find solace and strength in these supportive networks as they navigate their journey of healing.

For many victims seeking closure, acknowledgment of wrongdoing can be very healing and freeing, but gaining this may not always be possible or realistic. To move forward after parental abandonment without acknowledgment requires courage, resilience, and a willingness to confront painful truths. Reclaiming power and rewriting our own narratives, independent of our parent's presence or absence, is a journey of self-discovery and self-compassion. Still, it places additional burdens on survivors as we try to heal.

Convincing yourself that you are not to blame and you deserve to heal takes time. When natural feelings—such as anger, self-blame, and shame—present roadblocks in your healing journey, refer back to your notes from chapter 5 for support in moving through them.

Here are some additional strategies for helping to navigate this difficult area of healing:

- **Validate from within:** Self-validation involves acknowledging the pain and trauma you experienced and giving yourself permission to feel these while recognizing your strength in overcoming adversity. Regardless of whether the person who abandoned you acknowledges their actions, your feelings are valid, and it can be empowering to simply say (internally or out loud), *I feel angry, and I have every right to feel this way* to validate those experiences and emotions.

- **Find closure elsewhere:** Closure doesn't always have to come from the person who caused the harm; we can find it within us or through other sources of support and healing. Engage in rituals or ceremonies symbolizing closure, or find closure through creative outlets like visual art, music, or writing. At the end of this chapter, I include an exercise in which you write letters to the parent who left, which has been helpful for many of my clients seeking closure.

- **Cultivate self-compassion:** I encourage you to practice self-compassion for your own well-being. You deserve kindness and understanding, especially from yourself, even if this can feel difficult at times. Remember that healing is a journey that takes time and patience.

- **Foster healthy relationships:** I also encourage survivors to surround themselves with supportive and nurturing relationships. Healthy relationships can provide love, validation, and understanding—all things that you are likely lacking due to your abandonment. Building connections with chosen family and friends who respect and uplift you can be instrumental in your healing journey.

Moving forward without acknowledgment from the person who abandoned you is challenging, but healing and growth are still possible when you reclaim your power and create a brighter future for yourself. Next, we will explore reconciliation—a desire to reconnect and repair that may be closely aligned with the desire for acknowledgment of your experiences. We will explore the "why" behind a desire for reconciliation, and the likelihood that this may never happen.

What About Reconciliation?

Some people never feel any inclination to reach out to the parent who abandoned them. If you find yourself unable to relate to this section's title or first few sentences, this is absolutely normal. If you have no desire for reconciliation, this is fine, and I want to validate that experience. Feel free to skim this section to get an idea of what others may be experiencing and then move on when you feel ready. Keep in mind that reading it may be useful in highlighting additional elements of closure. For some, the one who abandoned you may have passed already, negating any possibility of reconciliation (if this if you, feel free to skip to the section titled "The Complexity of Grief After Abandonment").

Survivors of parental abandonment often ask, "Should I reach out?" This urge to make contact with the parent who left them can be stronger during triggering moments. These feelings can manifest in different ways, and there are many ways to go about handling those different experiences.

Reaching out to a parent who abandoned you can carry so many heavy emotions—the thought alone can be extremely traumatic. Simply wanting to reach out may come with feelings of isolation and being misunderstood, just as our realizing that there is no point to reaching out or that we have no desire to do so can trigger negative emotions. There is also a serious risk of emotional damage that can result from reaching out, especially if you try and are denied, refused, or rejected. Like many survivors, I can relate to the latter.

In my experience with this kind of retraumatization, I felt alone, isolated, and scared. Like many survivors, I had no idea how to handle the feelings that came up at the time. We are only recently starting to have public conversations around experiences of family trauma, especially from parental abandonment or family estrangement, and we're still figuring out the best ways to navigate it. Many of my clients describe having a sense of nowhere to go for help because so few of those they might turn to understand their experience. Those unable to relate might see reaching out as a simple task: you reach out, the one who abandoned you responds, and all is good. Naturally, they might have a hard time imagining a parent rejecting their child, because rejecting a child is not normal.

To abandon a child, most parents must first be able to justify that decision, often by any means necessary. As a result, they have prepared a strong defense against anyone who might accuse them of wrongdoing. When confronted with something we did wrong, whether we did it or not, it's natural to react defensively. Still, to a survivor still trying to heal, who has already struggled through gathering the strength to reach out in the first place, their parent's defensiveness and excuses—or worse, blame and further rejection—can feel more retraumatizing than their original act of abandonment.

I am not in *any* way advising you to not reach out, if reaching out is what you want to do. Every decision made while enduring the strong and conflicting feelings of abandonment is a personal one that only the individual survivor can make. When we have been wronged, I believe all of us hope for our moment in the sun—for survivors, that is a parent who listens to their feelings and experiences and owns up to what they did. If you share this hope, I have no desire to take it away from you. Still, I must mention that this ideal experience rarely comes to pass. Either way, I want to arm you with the tools to make the decision that is best for you and your healing journey.

Maybe you've already attempted to reach out before reading this section and you experienced the pain of retraumatization. Or maybe you read this section, knew the risks, and decided to reach out anyway. I make no judgments—it is only natural and human to want to contact our parents or caregivers and seek their support, even when they act inappropriately.

To anyone still thinking they might want to reach out to the parent who abandoned them, I offer the advice someone once gave me: "There is no statute of limitations on your decision. You can always change your mind later." Wanting to reach out does not mean you have to go back to page one and start over! Instead, you can focus on what matters most—healing. Continue pursuing efforts to repair from your traumas, and leave the decision whether to reach out on the table. Then, if you come back to it at some point further down the line and still want to reach out, you will likely be more healed and in a better position to deal with it.

If and when you take this road, or if you choose never to reach out at all, remember—this chapter will be here to help you deal with it.

Is Forgiveness Mandatory?

Just like reconciliation and moving forward without acknowledgment, conversations around forgiveness are common in the survivor community. Some experts tout forgiveness as critical to the healing process, but while it can be powerful for some, it is by no means mandatory for healing. Especially for survivors of abandonment and abuse, the topic is far more nuanced.

The wounds inflicted by abandonment run deep, and the pressure to forgive often sends victim-blaming messages. Many survivors find it impossible to forgive the person responsible for abandoning them. The pressure to forgive is often there for all survivors, but especially for marginalized and discriminated groups—women, LGBTQ+ people, and BIPOC, who are more frequently exposed to the effects of social and cultural conditioning—that pressure to forgive those who wronged them may be heavier, both internally and externally, and may involve more complex and painful emotions. Expecting all survivors to simply forgive and forget without considering their experiences feels like one more hurdle on their healing journey.

Rather than a requirement for healing, think of forgiveness as simply one possible outcome among many. As you work through your pain, you may start to find inner peace—a place of understanding and compassion that extends to the person who abandoned you. For some survivors, forgiveness may eventually emerge as a natural outgrowth of their healing journey. But although this can be true for some survivors, it is not essential for healing.

Healing is a deeply personal and independent journey with no one-size-fits-all approach. The outcome of this path will be different for each of us. Whether forgiveness plays a role should be a personal decision, free from external pressure or expectations.

If you are feeling any pressure to forgive, then it should likely not be part of your healing journey right now. Instead, prioritize mourning and a space to grieve the loss, process the pain, and heal. This may involve acknowledging and validating feelings of anger, betrayal, and sadness while resisting the pressure to forgive prematurely. To navigate your individual healing journey in a way that feels authentic and empowering to you, honor those emotions and experiences.

The Complexity of Grief After Abandonment

As we've discussed, survivors often struggle with feelings of grief after being abandoned by a parent or caregiver. Unfortunately, many survivors also have to navigate the added experience of additional feelings of grief when that parent dies. If you cannot relate to this section or have no interest in reading it, feel free to move on to the next. However, I encourage you to skim through to learn more about how this experience might impact you in the future, or bookmark and revisit it later.

Grieving the loss of a parent is always difficult, and the feelings of grief that result from an experience like the death of an important figure in your life can never really be replicated or compared to other losses. However, when someone who was abandoned by their parent then has to endure that parent's death, the grief over their death can feel like an even heavier burden than that borne when death ends a healthy, loving relationship. The grief over death is compounded by the initial grief over abandonment, as well as overwhelming feelings of guilt, shame, remorse, and resentment over what could or should have been, but never was, and a sense of permanent loss. Many find themselves riddled with self-doubt and self-blame, asking, "What if I had reached out…" or "I should have forgiven them," or other thoughts that compound the unfairness of their situation.

My client Sherry put it this way: "I feel so guilty saying I'm grieving the loss of my mother because I had no contact with her for the past decade before she died. My partner lost her mother last year, and they were so close. It's not the same at all! Am I still allowed to grieve?"

Maybe you had hoped for a reconciliation and now struggle with guilt or anger over the finality of its being too late. Maybe you never wanted a reconciliation, but the permanence that came with the loss of death reinforced the loss you had already experienced. What could have been is now impossible, leaving you feeling guilty, remorseful, or even resentful over their death.

The questions and judgments of others can make the parent's death all the more difficult for the survivor to navigate. Someone who has never been estranged from or abandoned by a caregiver could never understand the feelings that might come up for survivors of estrangement during this time; as a result, they can make insensitive, victim-blaming comments, such as:

"You must be relieved."

"Why are you sad? I thought you were upset with them."

"Well, you didn't talk anyway, so it can't be that hard."

"Don't you wish now that you had reached out?"

When they make comments that blame the survivor of abandonment for their estrangement, even if inadvertently, they can drive an already vulnerable and often traumatized individual to retraumatization and negative feelings like shame, anger, and resentment. As one client described it, "I don't even have the luxury of grieving like others have. Instead, I am juggling all of these other feelings of my abandonment before I can even get to the feeling of grief!"

Dealing with the grief that results from losing a parent who also abandoned you is quite different from the assumed grief after a close relative dies, and it's hard to know what feelings to prepare for. But while there may not be a one-size-fits-all solution for navigating the emotions that may come up, there are some general techniques that can help. Here are five actions to help you navigate that grief experience:

- **Validate and honor your feelings.** Outsiders who view family estrangement from a distance may make insensitive comments like those previously listed to invalidate your experience. Ignore them! You have every right to feel sad, angry, resentful, or even guilty. You neither owe anyone an explanation for these emotions nor need permission to feel them. No matter what you are feeling—shame, embarrassment, disappointment—allow yourself to acknowledge and validate those feelings. By honoring those feelings instead of letting others invalidate them, you set yourself up to manage them in a healthy way.

- **Practice self-compassion.** When survivors encounter negative feelings during the grieving process, they often think this indicates some admission of blame for their experience. These feelings might make you worry that you were wrong, that the estrangement was your fault, or that doing something differently would have prevented it. Acknowledge these feelings, but know that they are unfair and unrealistic and in no way imply that the experiences you remember never happened. Instead, take a moment and comfort yourself. You did nothing wrong.

- **Stick with people who provide a high level of support.** During your grieving process, you need people who are in your corner, not those who will challenge your feelings or make you feel misunderstood and uncomfortable, or as though you have to "prove" your grief. Choose instead to spend time with those who validate you and your feelings—sympathetic friends, family, support groups, or anyone who understands.

- **Remember that grief will come and go.** There will be good days, good weeks, and then just when you think you have felt your last pang of grief, a familiar song or smell drags you right back into grieving. This is normal, and being able to ride that ebb and flow is a part of healing.

- **Know when to seek out professional support.** Navigating grief is difficult, and any sort of dysfunction in the family relationship can make it much more complex. Rather than resolving or removing that dysfunction, the death of a parent or family member can leave even more dysfunction in its wake with the permanence of unanswered messages, unhealed traumas, and the resulting grief. No one is equipped to tackle these burdens alone, so if you find yourself without adequate support, a therapist or mental health professional can help.

Activity: Moving Forward

It's time to write a letter to little you (who was abandoned) from adult (present) you.

Step 1

As part of your healing journey, take a moment to connect with your inner child who experienced abandonment. Open your journal to a fresh page and begin by writing a heartfelt letter from your present self to the younger you who felt alone and lost. In your letter, offer words of comfort, understanding, and encouragement, acknowledging the pain of the past while also celebrating the strength and resilience you possess today. Allow yourself to express the love and compassion you deserve, bridging the gap between past and present as you nurture your inner child toward healing and wholeness.

For the main part of the letter, you are welcome to follow some of the prompts provided here, or you can just start writing and see what comes up for you—there is no right or wrong answer or direction to go in!

"Your abandonment was not your fault..."

"I know you are sad and scared, but..."

"You did not deserve to be abandoned..."

"I am writing to you from the future to tell you that you will be okay, even though it is scary right now..."

Step 2

When you're finished, wrap up the letter by saying how you are taking care of yourself. Write something similar to the following statement:

"As an adult, I take back my self-power and self-love, and I give up the shame that you have held onto. The abandonment was not your fault, but you held onto it; I release you from that, as it was never your shame to begin with."

In this chapter, we've explored the difficulty of moving forward without acknowledgment, pondered the possibility of reconciliation, and explored the notion of forgiveness as a requirement as well as the intricacies of grief after abandonment. Now, as we prepare to turn the page to our final chapter, I want you to stop and take a moment to commend yourself for coming this far. As I have said many times, healing is hard work, and examining your history of abandonment and resulting pain is not easy, but you are here, and you are doing the work! I am proud of you. Keep this in mind as we navigate the terrain of moving forward.

CHAPTER 9

Moving Forward

It was then that she realized there would be no answer good enough to explain the damage her mother had wrought by leaving her.

—Caroline Frost, *Shadows of Pecan Hollow*

Connie came to me for help in dealing with crippling feelings of shame and anxiety. She had gotten married just a few years ago and her parents had cut her out of their lives. "They didn't approve of my marrying someone outside of the faith," she told me.

Because she was an adult, people dismissed her parents' abandonment of her as just a simple family rift. Had she been a child, they might have been less likely to assign blame to her. She often experienced denial and gaslighting from friends and extended family who didn't understand the dynamics of the situation and continued to refer to the situation as her parents and her "not getting along." There was pressure for her to forgive them, to "come to an understanding," or even to "just move on." In every scenario, she was given as much responsibility as her parents to mend or maintain the relationship. This refusal to call what had happened abandonment fueled her confusion and pain, which crept up often as she tried to heal and live her life.

Why They Call It the "Work" of Healing

Healing is hard work. It is exhausting, painful, and frustrating, and it can feel hopeless and impossible at times. It can feel worse before it gets better. But I want to emphasize again that it is possible, and it is worth it.

When many people start the healing process, they take inventory of how little support they had during their traumatic experience. As Connie experienced, it is likely that extended family and friends reinforced your pain in some way. Like many others, you may have second-guessed your experiences when you got no support from a healthy adult to confirm that your abandonment was wrong.

Healing demands immense courage, resilience, and patience from those who embark upon it. At times, healing can feel like trudging through thick mud, each step weighed down by the burden of past traumas and unresolved emotions. Sometimes, this process can feel painfully slow, marked by setbacks and moments of despair. Years or even decades can go by in which we feel like we haven't made much progress. It's not uncommon for wounds to feel more raw and emotions more intense as healing begins to take root. It's as if the scars of the past are being reopened, exposing vulnerabilities that were long buried. Doubt may whisper that true healing is unattainable, or that wounds will always linger beneath the surface.

Yes, healing is challenging. It means confronting buried pain and making peace with forgotten parts of ourselves. It requires being vulnerable and honest and embracing discomfort. But it's worth it.

The healing journey is transformative. It reveals newfound joys in simple pleasures, enhances self-contentment, and deepens genuine relationships. So, I say to all of those struggling, remember: It may be hard and exhausting, but it is possible and worth it. Keep moving forward, reaching out for support, and holding onto hope. Healing, no matter how difficult, is always within reach.

This next section will discuss some of the most common aspects of healing that can feel overwhelming—those things that people mean when they discuss the "work" of healing.

Emotional Flashbacks: Common Obstacles to Healing

In the course of your healing journey, it's common to encounter obstacles—roadblocks that can disrupt the smooth flow of progress, much like unexpectedly encountering a barrier while driving. However, similar to encountering a roadblock, these difficulties are usually temporary setbacks that don't necessarily impede your overall progress. Instead, they often require taking a moment to pause, regroup, use your coping skills, and determine the best way to proceed.

In chapter 6, we discussed emotional triggers—external stimuli or situations that remind us of past traumatic events, causing us to react with heightened emotional intensity. Like triggers, emotional flashbacks also evoke intense emotional responses, but to a different degree.

Emotional flashbacks are internal experiences characterized by a reactivation of past emotions associated with a trauma, such as your abandonment. Unlike traditional flashbacks, which involve a vivid reliving of traumatic events, emotional flashbacks primarily involve reexperiencing the intense emotions specifically. Because these consist of the emotions only, many survivors struggle to understand what is actually happening when they feel these intense emotions. They may say things like, "I don't know why I reacted so strongly" or "I lost my mind—I don't know what happened!" It is likely that you have experienced this, but perhaps did not realize what it was.

During an emotional flashback, you may feel overwhelmed by emotions such as fear, shame, or helplessness, without necessarily recalling specific memories or details of the traumatic event. These emotional flashbacks can be triggered by internal cues such as thoughts, beliefs, or sensations that mirror those you experienced during the original trauma. This experience can be distressing and disruptive to daily life. To help you learn to recognize and cope with them more effectively, I have included some tips later in this section.

Emotional flashbacks can manifest in various forms and may vary from person to person. Some common examples include:

- **Intense, overwhelming fear or panic without a clear explanation.** Survivors often report feeling intense feelings of fear or panic when faced with situations such as an argument with a friend or a meeting with a boss.

- **Intense feelings of shame, guilt, or worthlessness,** which may be disproportionate to the current situation.

- **A sudden sense of emotional detachment, dissociation, or numbness,** as if disconnected from oneself or the present moment.

- **Intense anger or rage,** sometimes seemingly out of proportion to the triggering event. Anger can be a positive force that propels survivors forward on their journey toward healing. However, sometimes anger can lead to destructive behaviors and further alienate us from our own healing journey.

- **An overwhelming sense of helplessness or hopelessness:** This is often reminiscent of past experiences where you felt unable to control or change the outcome of a situation, such as when your abandonment took place.

- **Vivid flashbacks or intrusive memories of past traumatic events,** which may be triggered by seemingly unrelated present-day stimuli. Some people report this happens when faced with memories of their abandonment, such as during anniversaries or after seeing pictures or hearing familiar music.

- **Distressing physical sensations** such as racing heartbeat, sweating, trembling, or shortness of breath. Often, these feelings are reminiscent of the physiological arousal experienced during the abandonment. Sometimes, survivors who were unable to feel these negative feelings, due to being either in survival mode or unaware of what was happening, these feelings may be delayed and show up in later years.

Emotional Flashback or Just a Passing Feeling?

I often tell clients that when you experience a feeling and can recognize or acknowledge it, then it is a feeling or experience. But it becomes a roadblock when it literally or figuratively stops you in your journey of healing. Some people may notice that feelings pass more easily and are usually tied to something they can recognize. Unlike regular negative feelings, emotional flashbacks are typically disproportionate to the current situation; you may have a sense of disorientation or dissociation or feeling overwhelmed by emotions.

When You Encounter a Roadblock

It's helpful to recognize that healing is not about erasing the past or denying the pain—rather, it's about acknowledging the pain with compassion and support. By confronting the obstacles to healing head-on and cultivating a mindset of self-compassion, you can pave the way for continued healing. Here are some ways to do that:

- **Acknowledge it as an obstacle:** Begin by recognizing obstacles for what they are: painful feelings that stand in the way of healing. This is why I often refer to them as roadblocks—they are annoying and often inconvenient, and they force us to stop and think about how to get around them. Denying that the roadblock is there will not help you get around it. Instead, take a moment and acknowledge what is happening. Acknowledging and validating negative feelings and roadblocks is a vital step in the journey of healing from parental abandonment. Rather than suppressing or denying these emotions, we can benefit from approaching them with compassion and understanding.

- **Take a moment to yourself.** This will look different for each of you. For some, it might be a quick acknowledgment and then focusing on how to move forward. For others, it means allowing yourself some time to feel the intensity of the feelings for a while before you can focus on how to get around the obstacle. Neither of these options is better or worse, and there is certainly nothing at all wrong or defective about you if you need to take some time to feel the feelings before moving forward!

- **Practice grounding:** Bringing yourself to the present moment helps to decrease the intensity of the emotions you are experiencing. To practice grounding, intentionally focus on your immediate surroundings and sensory experiences. Engage your senses by noticing the sights, sounds, smells, textures, and tastes around you. This helps anchor you in the present moment, providing a sense of stability and reducing the intensity of emotional reactions. Remember your perfect protector, and use them for support!

- **Express gratitude to these roadblocks for making you stop and think.** I know this one might seem silly or even absurd. But by recognizing that these negative roadblocks have served you as protective mechanisms in response to past trauma, you can begin to untangle the roots of these feelings and reclaim agency over them. Start by expressing gratitude for the role these emotions play in safeguarding you against further pain. Because these feelings usually creep in as a way to prevent you from moving forward in your healing at a steady pace, it may seem like they are doing anything *but* trying to protect you. But they actually *are* trying to protect you—from experiencing these feelings or experiences again. Instead of trying to push them away, try expressing gratitude as you acknowledge them. This could be: *Thank you, anger, for showing me how I was wronged and hurt* or *Thank you for trying to protect me from being hurt again.* Expressing gratitude in this manner not only acknowledges the feeling but also reinforces grounding yourself in the present moment and allowing yourself to be present in the associated emotions.

- **Practice self-compassion:** This can be a powerful way to shift the narrative away from self-blame. By inviting these feelings to coexist alongside your desire for healing and growth, you can foster a more compassionate and accepting relationship with yourself.

Pete Walker, a psychotherapist and author specializing in complex trauma, notes the importance of recognizing and validating emotional flashbacks as a natural response to past trauma. He emphasizes that emotional flashbacks are not a sign of weakness or failure but rather a normal and understandable reaction to overwhelming experiences (Walker 2013). Additionally, Walker highlights the role of self-compassion and self-soothing techniques in managing emotional flashbacks. He encourages individuals to practice self-care activities to help regulate their emotions and bring themselves back to the present moment during a flashback.

Difficulty Opening Up and Trusting Others

In my experience working with survivors of parental abandonment, I rarely come across anyone who's had the experience of being able to openly and honestly share their feelings with an adult, either someone in their family or even an outside safe adult. Perhaps having this experience would have helped decrease their trauma and the aftermath. Instead, survivors of parental abandonment have usually lacked opportunities to openly and honestly express their feelings to a supportive adult figure. This lack of validation and understanding can exacerbate feelings of isolation and amplify the impact of the trauma.

It's likely that not having a safe space to express anger, sadness, or confusion still impacts you in adulthood. It can leave you feeling silenced and invalidated, further complicating the healing process. This underscores the importance of finding healthy outlets for expression and seeking support from trusted individuals or therapists who can provide a compassionate and nonjudgmental space where you can process emotions. With the following exercise, you can take time to practice the acknowledgment and compassion that you likely did not have when your abandonment happened. By acknowledging the significance of this unmet need and seeking out alternative avenues for validation and support, you are continuing on the path toward healing. Overcoming these obstacles requires a shift in perspective and a commitment to cultivating self-compassion and self-forgiveness—two critical supports that you have likely spent years or even decades avoiding. Many of us struggle to even know what it feels like to engage in caring approaches such as self-forgiveness or to have compassion and empathy for ourselves. So, at first, this concept may feel uncomfortable or foreign. But with practice, it will get easier. This next exercise will help you begin to practice.

Exercise: What Would You Say to a Friend?

We tend to be more harsh on ourselves than we are on others who are going through something similar. Therefore, as part of this process, it is helpful to imagine what you would say to someone else who is going through the same situation. By doing so, you can learn to extend the same kindness and understanding to yourself that you would offer to a cherished friend or loved one.

When you experience a roadblock, imagine a friend or loved one coming to you with *their* story and sharing *their* own roadblocks. What would you say to the friend? You likely would offer them compassion and kindness. At the very least, you likely would not blame them or reinforce their pain. Reflecting on what you would say to someone else can help you realize how hard you are on yourself.

Get out your journal and run through one or two of the following examples to help you practice:

- A friend comes to you and shares that they are feeling guilty and experiencing self-blame for thinking about what happened to them and how this may be affecting their children: "I feel bad that my kids don't get to have healthy relationships with their grandparents like other kids their age. I worry that it's my fault."

- A loved one shares that lately he has been experiencing a lot of anger toward his mother for abandoning him. He is struggling to work through and get past this anger.

- A friend shares with you that she is feeling shame and embarrassment that her father will not be in the audience at her upcoming college graduation. She feels embarrassed sharing this with others, especially friends whose parents will be there.

Now, practice with the following steps:

1. What would you say to them? Practice writing your response.

2. Next, consider the words you wrote. Would you say something similar to yourself? If not, why not? Take a moment to explore what comes up for you. Many people may have thoughts that further reinforce self-blame, perhaps thinking that they don't deserve the same compassion or worrying that they are doing the wrong thing. It's worth exploring why you recognize that the friend is not to blame, yet you believe *you* are in your own situation.

3. Finally, keep these words in mind as you move through your healing journey. When you experience roadblocks or negative emotions that come up, take a moment to give yourself grace and compassion. Perhaps borrow something from what you wrote down that you would say to a friend.

Reminders for the Healing Process

As you continue on your healing journey, I wanted to give you some kind words—and also reminders—for what may lie ahead. Healing is not a linear process; it's more akin to a winding path with ups and downs, twists and turns. There will be moments of progress and breakthroughs, but there will also be setbacks and challenges along the way. Expect to encounter triggers and difficult emotions as you delve into the depths of your past experiences.

Remember to be patient and gentle with yourself during these times. Allow yourself the space to feel whatever emotions arise, knowing that they are all valid and part of the healing process. You have been given many tips and tools throughout this book that will be helpful for you as you continue in your healing.

It's worth repeating: Healing does not happen overnight. It takes time, effort, and dedication to work through past traumas and wounds. Be willing to commit to the journey, even when it feels daunting or overwhelming. Celebrate the small victories and milestones along the way, no matter how insignificant they may seem. Each step forward, no matter how small, brings you closer to a place of healing and wholeness.

Furthermore, understand that healing is not a destination—it's an ongoing, lifelong journey. Even as you make progress and experience healing in one area of your life, new challenges may arise and old wounds may resurface. This is all a natural part of the process. Embrace the journey as a continuous evolution of self-discovery and growth. And above all, have faith in your own resilience and strength. You are capable of healing, of finding peace and joy, and of living a life filled with love and fulfillment. Trust in yourself and in the journey ahead, knowing that you have the power to transform your pain into strength and your wounds into wisdom.

As you continue on your healing journey, keep these things in mind:

- **Practice self-compassion:** It is crucial to show yourself kindness and self-compassion, now and always. This gentle self-care approach can counteract feelings of shame and self-blame, promoting resilience and facilitating the journey toward healing and growth. Remember that we often speak to and about ourselves more harshly than we would to other survivors. Keep this in mind when you notice you're being hard on yourself, and try to go easier.

- **Keep learning and growing:** We are always learning more about ourselves as we heal. Keep learning and keep growing as you go along, by reading books such as this one, listening to podcasts, journaling, and finding other ways to continue healing.

- **Remember who is responsible and who isn't:** It can be so easy to slip into resentment with family, especially siblings and external family members who still have a relationship with the parent who left you. It helps to remember who is responsible (the parent who left you) and who is not (likely your siblings, cousins, or extended family who were powerless in the situation). It is perfectly okay to have any number of feelings about the situation, but try not to place blame where it is not deserved.

- **Remember that healing does not mean that all negative feelings go away!** It means only that you feel them more appropriately and are better equipped to deal with them when they come up.

Signs That You Are Healing

I'm often asked, "How will I know when I am healing?" I remember asking that same question myself, impatient and ready to stop feeling so many negative feelings.

Recognizing when you are healing is an essential aspect of the journey. Although healing is a deeply personal and individualized process, there are several common signs and indicators that may suggest progress along the way:

- **Increased self-awareness:** As you heal, you may find yourself becoming more self-aware and attuned to your emotions, thoughts, and behaviors.

- **Increased emotional resilience:** Healing often involves building emotional resilience—the ability to bounce back from setbacks and cope with life's challenges more effectively. You may notice yourself becoming better equipped to manage stress, regulate your emotions, and navigate difficult situations with greater ease.

- **Improved relationships:** As you heal from past wounds, you may find that your relationships with others improve. You may notice that you communicate more openly and authentically, have healthier boundaries, and cultivate deeper connections based on trust and mutual respect.

- **Greater sense of empowerment:** Healing empowers you to reclaim control over your life and choices. You may feel a renewed sense of agency and autonomy, as well as a greater willingness to advocate for your needs and pursue your goals.

- **Reduced symptoms:** Healing often leads to a reduction in symptoms associated with trauma or emotional distress. While it's normal to experience ups and downs along the way, you may notice a decrease in the frequency or intensity of symptoms such as anxiety, depression, or intrusive thoughts. Many survivors also notice a decrease in physical pains such as acid reflux, a lowering of blood pressure, and improved mobility and energy.

- **Increased joy and fulfillment:** As healing progresses, you may find yourself experiencing more moments of joy, peace, and fulfillment in your life. You may rediscover interests and activities that bring you pleasure as well as generate a greater sense of gratitude for the present moment.

- **Acceptance and forgiveness:** Healing often involves a process of acceptance and forgiveness—of both yourself and others. You may find yourself letting go of resentment and bitterness and instead embracing compassion and understanding.

Again, healing is not a linear process, and progress may be gradual and nonlinear. Despite the inevitable setbacks and challenges along the way, each step forward—no matter how small—will bring you closer to a place of healing and wholeness. Trust in your journey, and be gentle with yourself as you navigate the path toward healing. You have gained many tools and coping skills along the way, not only in reading this book, but likely in other areas of your life as well. Trust in yourself and remember to always show self-compassion.

Final Activity: My Toolbox for My Healing Journey

In this final activity, you have the opportunity to reflect on the various coping strategies and resources we explored in this book and to select the ones you can take with you for your healing journey.

Step 1. First, reflect on past experiences and everything we explored in this book and identify the coping strategies that have been most effective for you in managing difficult emotions and situations. This may include journaling, mindfulness exercises, creative expression, physical exercise, or seeking support from trusted friends or mental health professionals. Grab your notebook and start making a list.

Step 2. Next, call on your protective shield and/or your perfect protector that you created earlier in the book. Add this to your toolbox.

Step 3. Once you have compiled a list of potential tools and resources, create a visual representation of this toolbox, whether through drawing, collage, or writing. This visual representation can serve as a tangible reminder of the resources available to you, especially if you display it in a prominent place as a source of inspiration and motivation.

Step 4. Finally, take time to reflect on how you can actively incorporate these tools into your daily life and commit to using them as needed throughout your healing journey. This may involve creating a plan for incorporating self-care practices into your daily or weekly routine, reaching out for support when needed, and practicing self-compassion and self-acceptance.

Overall, this activity should serve as a powerful reinforcement of your healing journey, empowering you to take ownership of the healing process and equipping you with the tools and resources you need to navigate the challenges or difficulties that come up as you continue to heal.

Healing is hard work, but I am worth it.

Supplemental: How Partners and Loved Ones Can Best Support You

Loved ones can play a crucial role in supporting you on your journey of healing from parental abandonment. Their presence, understanding, and empathy can provide a valuable source of comfort and strength during difficult times. In my work with clients, many often ask how partners and other loved ones can get involved. I have written this supplement for them, but I also encourage you to read through it before handing it over, so you know what suggestions they've been given—and also what you can reasonably and realistically expect from them.

Here, speaking directly to your supporters, I offer several ways in which they can best support you in navigating the challenges of moving forward from parental abandonment:

- **Just listen:** First and foremost, you can offer a nonjudgmental space for survivors to express their feelings and experiences openly. Simply listening with empathy and validation can be incredibly comforting and reassuring for survivors, helping them feel seen, heard, and understood. You may worry that you don't know what to say, or don't know the perfect thing to say. I always recommend just listening actively to show that you are invested and supportive: nod and/or maintain eye contact; ask occasional follow-up questions; and avoid getting distracted by other tasks at hand.

- **Don't tell survivors that it's okay or it's not that bad:** As many survivors have spent years or even lifetimes having their experience of abandonment excused or denied, you can instead acknowledge the pain and complexity of parental abandonment without trying to minimize or fix it. Survivors of abandonment often have a history of being blamed for the events that took place, or they may carry internal blame and shame for having been abandoned. Simply showing that you believe them and expressing empathy can make a huge difference.

- **Education:** If you are interested, you can educate yourself about the impact of parental abandonment and trauma to better understand the challenges faced by survivors and how best to support them. This may involve reading books, attending workshops, or seeking guidance from mental health professionals. By becoming an informed ally, you can offer more effective support and validation while also avoiding inadvertently triggering or retraumatizing the survivor. This self-education is not necessary by any means but can be helpful for some.

- **Keep proper boundaries.** There is a difference between listening to show support, and being cast in the role of therapist or "fixer," which is inappropriate and unrealistic. If you are noticing that the survivor is struggling, it is okay to suggest that they may need a mental health professional to help them work through some of their past.

Further Resources and Support for Healing

Books on Family of Origin Trauma

Bradshaw, J. 2005. *Healing the Shame That Binds You.* Deerfield Beach, FL: HCI Books.

Maté, G. 2022. *The Myth of Normal: Trauma, Illness, and Healing in a Toxic Culture.* New York: Penguin Books.

Perry, B. D., and O. Winfrey. 2021. *What Happened to You?: Conversations on Trauma, Resilience, and Healing.* New York: Flatiron Books.

van der Kolk, B. A. 2014. *The Body Keeps the Score: Brain, Mind and Body in the Healing of Trauma.* New York: Penguin Books.

Walker, P. 2013. *Complex PTSD: From Surviving to Thriving,* 1st ed. Lafayette, CA: Azure Coyote.

Webb, J. 2012. *Running on Empty: Overcome Your Childhood Emotional Neglect.* Washington, DC: Morgan James Publishing.

Books on Attachment and Improving Relationships

Becker-Phelps, L. 2014. *Insecure in Love: How Anxious Attachment Can Make You Feel Jealous, Needy, and Worried and What You Can Do About It.* New York: New Harbinger Publications.

Lancer, D. 2014. *Conquering Shame and Codependency: 8 Steps to Freeing the True You.* New York: Simon and Schuster.

Tawwab, N. G. 2024. *The Drama Free Workbook: Practical Exercises for Managing Unhealthy Family Relationships.* Los Angeles: TarcherPerigee.

Books on Healing Trauma Responses

Durvasula, R. 2023. *It's Not You: Identifying and Healing from Narcissistic People.* New York: Penguin Books.

Maté, G., and D. Maté. 2018. *In the Realm of Hungry Ghosts: Close Encounters with Addiction.* Toronto: Vintage Canada.

Petrella, D. 2023. *Healing Emotional Eating for Trauma Survivors.* Oakland, CA: New Harbinger Publications.

Books on Healing from Abusive and Neglectful Caregivers

Arabi, S. 2019. *Healing the Adult Children of Narcissists: Essays on the Invisible War Zone and Exercises for Recovery and Reflection.* SCW Archer Publishing.

Fabrizio, K. 2023. *The Good Daughter Syndrome: Help for Empathic Daughters of Narcissistic, Borderline, or Difficult Mothers Trapped in the Role of the Good Daughter.* New York: Simon & Schuster.

Gibson, L. 2015. *Adult Children of Emotionally Immature Parents.* New York: New Harbinger Publications.

Hill, L. 2022. *Recovery from Narcissistic Abuse, Gaslighting, Codependency and Complex PTSD (4 Books in 1): Workbook and Guide to Overcome Trauma, Toxic Relationships, Anxiety, and Improve Mental Health.* San Francisco: Peak Publish LLC.

Mason, P. T., and R. Kreger. 2010. *Walking on Eggshells: Navigating the Delicate Relationship Between Adult Children and Parents.* Oakland, CA: New Harbinger Publications.

Acknowledgments

This book's intent and message began years after my initial experiences of neglect and abandonment had settled enough for me to be able to acknowledge what had happened enough to work through it. I owe my first thanks to my therapist, Dena, who helped me heal, and who likely contributed to who I am today—someone who uses my story to heal and uplift others.

To those who stood by me when I was unhealed and during my healing journey, thank you. It can't be easy to support someone in pain.

To those who read my words in *Psychology Today*, *Psychotherapy Networker*, and other sources, and those who have read my previous books, thank you. All of you remind me why I do what I do, and you all keep me passionate about writing about healing.

Thank you to my acquisitions editor, Elizabeth Hollis Hansen, for supporting my passion for this topic; my coordinating editor, Madeline Greenhalgh; my copyeditor, Kristi Hein; and my publicist, Analis Souza; and to all of you at New Harbinger, for believing in my message and for being both supportive of my writing and passionate about the need for this book.

Thank you to:

Juan, for your support and love, and for always showing me the best in myself—I am lucky to have a partner like you.

Mom, for always supporting my writing.

Will and Stacy, for your continued support and understanding.

Talon, for unwavering friendship and support.

Grace, for always helping me with getting my message out there.

Clara and Mark, for supporting and leading me toward healing and growth.

Those who have come into my life, friends near and far, who have encouraged and supported me, both in my healing and in my aims to help others.

My fur kids, Gomez and Binx, for teaching me unconditional love, and keeping me company as I write...and reminding me of the importance of regular snacks!

References

Bath, H. 2019. "Pain and the Unspoken Emotion: Shame." *International Journal of Child, Youth and Family Studies* 10(3): 126–141.

Bradshaw, J. 2005. *Healing the Shame That Binds You*. Deerfield Beach, FL: HCI Books.

Chapman, B., K. Fiscilla, I. Kawachi, P. Duberstein, and P. Muenning. 2013. "Emotion Suppression and Mortality Risk Over a 12-Year Follow-Up." *Journal of Psychosomatic Research* August 6. https://www.ncbi.nlm.nih.gov/pmc/articles/PMC3939772.

Ellis, B. J., N. Shakiba, D. E. Adkins, and B. M. Lester. 2020. « Early External, Environmental, and Internal Health Predictors of Risky Sexual and Aggressive Behavior in Adolescence: An Integrative Approach." *Developmental Psychology* 63(3): 556–571.

Elsig, C. 2022. "The Dangers of Suppressing Emotions." Calda Clinic, January 24. https://caldaclinic.com/dangers-of-suppressing-emotions.

Felitti, V. J., R. F. Anda, D. Nordenberg, D. F. Williamson, A. M. Spitz, V. Edwards, M. P. Koss, and J. S. Marks. 1998. "Relationship of Childhood Abuse and Household Dysfunction to Many of the Leading Causes of Death in Adults: The Adverse Childhood Experiences (ACE) Study." *American Journal of Preventive Medicine* 14(4): 245–258.

Grossarth-Maticek, R., J. Bastiaans, and D. T. Kanazir. 1985. "Psychosocial Factors as Strong Predictors of Mortality from Cancer, Ischaemic Heart Disease and Stroke: The Yugoslav Prospective Study." *Journal of Psychosomatic Research*. https://pubmed.ncbi.nlm.nih.gov/4009517.

Tello, M. 2019. "A Positive Mindset Can Help Your Heart." *Harvard Health Publishing* March 6. https://www.health.harvard.edu/blog /a-positive-mindset-can-help-your-heart-2019021415999.

Harvard T. H. Chan School of Public Health. 2011. "Finding Happiness May Protect Your Heart." *Harvard T. H. Chan School of Public Health.* www.hsph.harvard.edu/news/magazine/happiness-stress-heart-disease.

Harvard University Center on the Developing Child. (n.d.). *Neglect.* https://developingchild.harvard.edu/science/deep-dives/neglect.

Jennings, A., and R. Ralph. "Community Retraumatization." In "In Their Own Words: Trauma Survivors and Professionals They Trust Tell What Hurts, What Helps, and What Is Needed for Trauma Services." The Anna Institute. https://www.theannainstitute.org/articles.html.

Lorijn, S., M. Engels, M. Huisman, and R. Veenstra. 2021. "Long-Term Effects of Acceptance and Rejection by Parents and Peers on Educational Attainment: A Study from Pre-Adolescence to Early Adulthood." *Journal of Youth and Adolescence* 51: 540–555. https://link.springer.com/article/10.1007/s10964-021-01506-z.

Lim, C. R., and J. Barlas. 2019. "The Effects of Toxic Early Childhood Experiences on Depression According to Young Schema Model: A Scoping Review." *Journal of Affective Disorders* 246: 1–13.

Lancer, D. 2014. *Conquering Shame and Codependency: 8 Steps to Freeing the True You.* New York: Simon & Schuster.

Morris, M. C., N. Hellman, J. L. Abelson, and U. Rao. 2016. "Cortisol, Heart Rate, and Blood Pressure as Early Markers of PTSD Risk: A Systematic Review and Meta-analysis." *Clinical Psychology Review* 49: 79–91. https://doi.org/10.1016/j.cpr.2016.09.001.

Marici, M., O. Clipa, R. Runcan, and L. Pîrghie. 2023. "Is Rejection, Parental Abandonment or Neglect a Trigger for Higher Perceived Shame and Guilt in Adolescents?" *Healthcare* (*Basel*) 11(12), June 12: 1724. https://doi.org/10.3390/healthcare11121724.

Maté, G. 2022. *The Myth of Normal: Trauma, Illness, and Healing in a Toxic Culture*. New York: Penguin Books.

Nwanaji-Enwerem, U., E. O. Onsomu, D. Roberts, et al. 2022. "Relationship Between Psychosocial Stress and Blood Pressure: The National Heart, Lung, and Blood Institute Family Heart Study." *SAGE Open Nursing* 8, June 23. https://doi.org/10.1177/237796 08221107589.

Patel, J., and P. Prittesh. 2019. "Consequences of Repression of Emotion: Physical Health, Mental Health and General Well Being." *International Journal of Psychotherapy Practice and Research*. https://doi.org/10.14302 /issn.2574-612X.ijpr-18-2564.

Perry, B. D., and O. Winfrey. 2021. *What Happened to You?: Conversations on Trauma, Resilience, and Healing*. Unabridged. New York: Flatiron Books.

Quartana, P. J., and J. W. Burns. 2010. "Emotion Suppression Affects Cardiovascular Responses to Initial and Subsequent Laboratory Stressors." *British Journal of Health Psychology*. https://pubmed.ncbi .nlm.nih.gov/19840496.

Rigas, H. M., S. Bucur, D. M. Ciurduc, I. E. Nita, and M. M. Constantin. 2019. "Psychological Stress and Depression in Psoriasis Patients: A Dermatologist's Perspective." *Maedica (Bucur)* 14(3): 287–291. doi:10.26574/maedica.2019.14.3.287.

Schilling, E. A., R. H. Aseltine Jr, and S. Gore. 2007. "Adverse Childhood Experiences and Mental Health in Young Adults: A Longitudinal Survey." *BMC Public Health*.

Substance Abuse and Mental Health Services Administration (SAMHSA). 2017. "Tips for Survivors of a Disaster or Other Traumatic Event: Coping with Retraumatization." Substance Abuse and Mental Health Services Administration. https://store.samhsa .gov/sites/default/files/sma17-5047.pdf.

Symonides, B., P. Holas, M. Schram, J. Śleszycka, A. Bogaczewicz, and Z. Gaciong. 2014. "Does the Control of Negative Emotions Influence Blood Pressure Control and Its Variability?" *Blood Pressure* December PMID: 24786662. https://pubmed.ncbi.nlm.nih.gov/24786662 /#:~:text=Conclusion.,%3B%20anxiety%3B%20depression%3B %20hypertension.

Taylor, S. E. 2011. "Social Support: A Review." In *The Oxford Handbook of Health Psychology*, edited by H. S. Friedman (189–214). Oxford University Press. https://doi.org/10.1093/oxfordhb/9780195342819 .013.0010.

Teachman, J. D. 2004. "The Childhood Living Arrangements of Children and the Characteristics of Their Marriages." *Journal of Family Issues* 25(1): 86–111.

van der Kolk, B. A. 2014. *The Body Keeps the Score: Brain, Mind and Body in the Healing of Trauma*. New York: Penguin Books.

Wang, F., Y. Gao, Z. Han, Y. Yu, Z. Long, X. Jiang, Y. Wu, B. Pei, Y. Cao, J. Ye, M. Wang, and Y. Zhao. 2023. "A Systematic Review and Meta-analysis of 90 Cohort Studies of Social Isolation, Loneliness and Mortality." *Nature Human Behaviour* August 7(8): 1307–1319. doi: 10.1038/s41562-023-01617-6. PMID: 37337095.

Walker, P. 2013. *Complex PTSD: From Surviving to Thriving*, 1st ed. Lafayette, CA: Azure Coyote.

Webb, J. 2018. "How to Overcome Abandonment Issues from Childhood." DrJoniceWebb.com. May 22. https://drjonicewebb.com /the-3-main-issues-of-the-abandoned-child-in-adulthood/.

Kaytlyn "Kaytee" Gillis, LCSW, is a psychotherapist and author with a passion for working with survivors of relationship and family trauma, and with the LGBTQ+ community. Her work focuses on assisting survivors and educating clinicians and the public about the effects of psychological family trauma. She has published several books and contributed to many others, and provides trainings nationwide.

Kaytee's work has been featured in *TIME, BBC World News, The Dr. Wendy Walsh Show, CP24 News,* and many other outlets. She is a regular contributor to *Psychotherapy Networker,* and writes the popular column "Invisible Bruises" for *Psychology Today.* An avid traveler, Kaytee enjoys trying the local coffee wherever she goes. She lives with her partner and two fur children.

Foreword writer **Elaine Miller-Karas, LCSW,** is cofounder and executive director emeritus of the Trauma Resource Institute (TRI). Miller-Karas is a psychotherapist, and author of *Building Resilience to Trauma.* She shares her expertise with the public through her contributions to *Psychology Today,* and through her weekly radio show, *Resiliency Within,* on VoiceAmerica.

Real change *is* possible

For more than fifty years, New Harbinger has published proven-effective self-help books and pioneering workbooks to help readers of all ages and backgrounds improve mental health and well-being, and achieve lasting personal growth. In addition, our spirituality books offer profound guidance for deepening awareness and cultivating healing, self-discovery, and fulfillment.

Founded by psychologist Matthew McKay and Patrick Fanning, New Harbinger is proud to be an independent, employee-owned company. Our books reflect our core values of integrity, innovation, commitment, sustainability, compassion, and trust. Written by leaders in the field and recommended by therapists worldwide, New Harbinger books are practical, accessible, and provide real tools for real change.

 **newharbinger**publications

MORE BOOKS from
NEW HARBINGER PUBLICATIONS

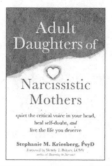
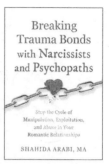
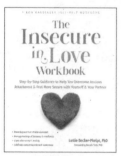

Did you know there are **free tools** you can download for this book?

Free tools are things like **worksheets, guided meditation exercises**, and **more** that will help you get the most out of your book.

You can download free tools for this book— whether you bought or borrowed it, in any format, from any source—from the New Harbinger website. All you need is a NewHarbinger.com account. Just use the URL provided in this book to view the free tools that are available for it. Then, click on the "download" button for the free tool you want, and follow the prompts that appear to log in to your NewHarbinger.com account and download the material.

You can also save the free tools for this book to your **Free Tools Library** so you can access them again anytime, just by logging in to your account! Just look for this button on the book's free tools page.

+ Save this to my free tools library

If you need help accessing or downloading free tools, visit **newharbinger.com/faq** or contact us at **customerservice@newharbinger.com.**